THE ORIGINS OF THE
COLD WAR, 1941–1947

PROBLEMS IN AMERICAN HISTORY

EDITOR

LOREN BARITZ

State University of New York, Albany

THE LEADERSHIP OF ABRAHAM LINCOLN
Don E. Fehrenbacher

THE AMERICAN CONSTITUTION
Paul Goodman

THE AMERICAN REVOLUTION
Richard J. Hooker

AMERICA IN THE COLD WAR
Walter LaFeber

THE ORIGINS OF THE COLD WAR, 1941–1947
Walter LaFeber

AMERICAN IMPERIALISM IN 1898
Richard H. Miller

TENSIONS IN AMERICAN PURITANISM
Richard Reinitz

THE GREAT AWAKENING
Darrett B. Rutman

WORLD WAR I AT HOME
David F. Trask

THE CRITICAL YEARS,
AMERICAN FOREIGN POLICY, 1793–1825
Patrick C. T. White

THE ORIGINS OF THE COLD WAR, 1941–1947:

A Historical Problem with Interpretations and Documents

EDITED BY
Walter LaFeber
Cornell University

John Wiley & Sons, Inc.
New York · London · Sydney · Toronto

Library of Congress Catalogue Card Number: 76-142718

Cloth: ISBN 0-471-51140-4 Paper: ISBN 0-471-51141-2

Printed in the United States of America

10 9 8 7 6 5 4 3 2 1

SERIES PREFACE

This series is an introduction to the most important problems in the writing and study of American history. Some of these problems have been the subject of debate and argument for a long time, although others only recently have been recognized as controversial. However, in every case, the student will find a vital topic, an understanding of which will deepen his knowledge of social change in America.

The scholars who introduce and edit the books in this series are teaching historians who have written history in the same general area as their individual books. Many of them are leading scholars in their fields, and all have done important work in the collective search for better historical understanding.

Because of the talent and the specialized knowledge of the individual editors, a rigid editorial format has not been imposed on them. For example, some of the editors believe that primary source material is necessary to their subjects. Some believe that their material should be arranged to show conflicting interpretations. Others have decided to use the selected materials as evidence for their own interpretations. The individual editors have been given the freedom to handle their books in the way that their own experience and knowledge indicate is best. The overall result is a series built up from the individual decisions of working scholars in the various fields, rather than one that conforms to a uniform editorial decision.

A common goal (rather than a shared technique) is the bridge of this series. There is always the desire to bring the reader as close to these problems as possible. One result of this objective is an emphasis on the nature and consequences of problems and events, with a de-emphasis of the more purely historiographical issues. The goal is to involve the student in the reality of crisis, the inevitability of ambiguity, and the excitement of finding a way through the historical maze.

Above all, this series is designed to show students how experienced historians read and reason. Although health is not contagious, intellectual engagement may be. If we show students something significant in a phrase or a passage that they otherwise may have missed, we will have accomplished part of our objective. When students see something that passed us by, then the process will have been made whole. This active and mutual involvement of editor and reader with a significant human problem will rescue the study of history from the smell and feel of dust.

Loren Baritz

CONTENTS

CHAPTER III

Restructuring the British Empire

CHAPTER IV

Poland, the Symbol

Contents

THE ORIGINS OF THE
COLD WAR, 1941–1947

GERMANY IN DEFEAT

GENERAL INTRODUCTION

The Cold War resulted largely from the same problems that confront Americans today, more than twenty-five years later. Doubtless at least the entire last half of the twentieth century will be shaped by the tensions that developed between the United States and Russia during the first half of that century and particularly during the 1941–1947 period. The roots of that confrontation are complex, but if we hope to ameliorate the problems of the Cold War, both at home and abroad, the historical record must be understood. Each of us has some ideas about how and why our lives have been so moulded by the United States–Soviet conflict after World War II. It follows that we must understand that history as fully and as accurately as possible.

The United States and Russia first opposed one another in the 1890s when each nation sought to exploit China and Manchuria. It was a preview of the struggle a half century later: Americans hoped to keep Asia open to all nations on equal terms (the "Open Door"), while Russia, unable to compete on such terms with the more industrialized nations, sought to close off and privately develop certain areas.

The confrontation intensified considerably after the Bolsheviks gained control of Russia in late 1917. American policy makers had long feared the military and industrial potential of Russia, and after 1917 that fear was sharpened by a Soviet government that viewed itself as the vanguard of an ideological revolutionary movement that would transform international affairs. In 1918 the United States joined Great Britain and Japan to intervene in the Russian Revolution by sending military forces to occupy strategic points within the Soviet Union. This foreign intrusion, however, only increased the allegiance of the Russian people to the Bolsheviks. The State Department acted on this realization by withdrawing the American troops in 1920 and then announcing that it would not recognize the Bolshevik government as officially in existence.

In 1933 the United States finally recognized the Soviet Union, but throughout the next six years neither American nor Western European leaders sufficiently trusted Russia to cooperate with her in stopping German and Japanese aggression. In a speech of March 1939, Soviet ruler Josef Stalin interpreted the renewed economic depression in the West as evidence of that area's weakness, and concluded that the Munich agreement of September 1938 (in which Great Britain and France handed to Hitler a portion of Czechoslovakia without the Czechs' consent) was proof that the Western powers were attempting to turn Hitler's armies eastward toward Russia.

Five months after Stalin's speech, the Soviet leader and Hitler signed an agreement that allowed the German dictator to attack westward without fear of the Russians on his eastern flank. The pact also gave Stalin large sections of Poland and the Balkans as security buffers and for economic exploitation. The two dictators, however, soon began arguing over the proper division of the spoils. On June 22, 1941, Hitler attacked Russia. After a notable delay of twenty-four hours, the United States Department of State announced that it would help Stalin defend his country against the Nazis. The announcement, however, was less than enthusiastic; for example, it criticized the Soviets for not allowing full freedom of worship. The two great nations were now bound together in common cause, but the historical record indicated the flimsiness and weaknesses of those bonds.

Indeed, within months after Americans and Russians became partners against Hitler, they began having serious differences over post-war reconstruction policies. During the war, these differences were muted for the sake of the common military effort, but the tension between the two great powers did not abate. The key to understanding that tension and the resulting split between Russia and the United States was the different methods with which each nation planned to advance its own interests in the post-war world.

US aim   The United States wanted a world without power blocs or obstacles to trade, a world in which all nations, under the aegis of the United Nations, would enjoy equal opportunity and equal rights. In reality, Americans would be first among equals in such a world because of their overwhelming economic power and military potential. This vision was described vividly by the phrase, "The American Century," made popular in 1941 by Henry Luce, the founder and Editor-in-Chief of *Time and Life* magazines.

The Russians planned a quite different kind of world. They were weakened by war and were convinced both by Marxist-Leninist ideology and by the historical record of the 1917–1939 era that the Western capitalist nations had no intentions of preserving Soviet

interests. The Russians therefore wanted a world that would provide USSR aims
maximum security around their borders and as far into Europe and
Asia as possible. This security would necessarily include rapid reconstruction of the Soviets' war-devastated economy and would be
accompanied by the exploitation of bordering, occupied lands if no
other economic means were available.

The results were ironic and tragic. Within a decade the American
Century developed into a military ring of "containment" around the
Soviet bloc. The Russian quest for security resulted in encirclement
without and a totalitarian dictatorship within.

This volume attempts to trace the course of those tragedies during
the 1941–1947 period. It opens with two different interpretations,
written by well-known historians, which offer general and conflicting
views of why the Cold War developed during those years. The
remainder of the book offers contemporary documents against which
the student can check the general interpretations, and especially
develop views of his own warranted by the historical evidence. The
documents have been chosen to provide some insight into Soviet
as well as American motivations. Several of the sources used, such
as the Bernard Baruch papers at Princeton and some official State
Department records of 1945, have only recently been opened to
scholars. Instead of trying to cover all important diplomatic events,
the documents attempt first to reveal general policy considerations
(Chapter II), and then to move to several case studies that best
exemplify the conflict of Russian and American policies (Chapter III,
IV, and V). The book closes with materials which indicate the rigid-
ness and results of those policies by 1946 and 1947 when the Cold War
was an accepted fact by both sides.

CHAPTER I

TWO INTERPRETATIONS

1 FROM

Thomas A. Bailey
The Kremlin Did Not Want Agreement—
Except on Its Own Terms

For, more than thirty years a distinguished professor of history at Stanford, Thomas A. Bailey is also a dean of American diplomatic historians. His A Diplomatic History of the American People *is in its eighth edition as a textbook and has had immense influence in shaping American foreign policy classes in many colleges. In that textbook and in the selection from* America Faces Russia *that follows, two theses appear: a highly critical view of Soviet foreign policy and the assumption that American public opinion is important in defining United States foreign policy. Note particularly how Professor Bailey defines the causes of the Russian—American split in 1945; does he see these causes as primarily political, economic, or ideological? What role does public opinion play, either explicitly or implicitly, in the selections following Professor Bailey's essay?*

The aloof Soviets revealed no eagerness to take part in Allied conferences, whether major or minor. They even rejected an invitation in 1944 to attend the Chicago aviation conference on the pretext that "fascist" countries like Switzerland would be represented. So bad was the atmosphere in 1943 that the aged and ailing Secretary of State Hull, without vaccination or immunization, boarded an airplane for

US bias

SOURCE. Thomas A. Bailey, *America Faces Russia, Russian-American Relations From Early Times to Our Day.* (Ithaca, New York: Cornell University Press, 1950), pp. 312–327. Reprinted by special permission of the author.

the first time in his life and flew to Moscow, where he succeeded in producing an upswing in cordiality. President Roosevelt, after repeated efforts to bring about a meeting, twice risked his life in crossing the Atlantic to confer with Stalin at Teheran and then at Yalta.[1]

The standoffishness of our Slavic ally merely confirmed the worst suspicions of a host of Americans. But fair-minded observers perceived that Soviet unco-operativeness often stemmed from a desire to avoid provoking Japan. This was notably true of the Cairo conference, [in 1943] which was primarily concerned with prosecuting the war against the Nipponese and which, insofar as it related to the Far East, could not be attended by "neutral" Russia. Stalin, moreover, was absorbed with directing the defense of the U.S.S.R., and later the gigantic offensives that the Red army finally mounted. But a noisy and growing group of Americans felt, not altogether without reason, that the nonattendance or halfhearted participation of the Soviets sprang from a determination to pursue their own aims unilaterally, without regard for the common cause.

In February, 1945, Roosevelt, Churchill, and Stalin met at Yalta, a beautiful but Nazi-ravaged resort on the shores of the Crimea. This was the last gathering of the Big Three attended by the fast-failing Roosevelt, and in some ways it marked the high tide of inter-Allied co-operation. The conferees agreed on the destruction and shackling of Germany, as well as on a voting formula for the big powers at the forthcoming San Francisco Conference. The decisions *Poland* that aroused the most violent outcry at the time concerned Poland. Stalin pledged himself to support a more broadly based democratic government than that provided by either the Lublin or London factions. The new Poland was to be shorn of approximately the formerly Russian-owned eastern third, while compensating territory was to be torn from the side of Germany on the west.

These arrangements stirred up a veritable hornets' nest of criticism. The London Poles, as well as the Catholic and Polish groups in America, condemned the Yalta "betrayal." Poland, they charged, had been saved from her enemies only to be crucified by her friends. Congressman Lesinski of Michigan and Congressman O'Konski of

---

[1] The battleship carrying Roosevelt across the Atlantic to Teheran was almost struck accidentally by a torpedo, and his plane flying to Yalta was almost forced down in the mountains by ice. Admiral Leahy was convinced that Stalin could not leave the direction of the Soviet armies (W.D. Leahy, *I Was There* [New York, 1950], pp. 196, 296, 303).

Wisconsin assailed the "crime of Crimea" as a "stab in the back" for
Poland and as a "second Munich." A secret agreement at Yalta, which
leaked out prematurely the next month and caused strong reactions in
the United States, stipulated that both the U.S.S.R. and the United
States, as an offset to the six votes of the British Commonwealth, might
seek three votes in the Assembly of the projected world organization.
Washington promptly renounced any such pretension, but Russia
ultimately secured one vote for herself and an additional vote for
the Ukraine and White Russia.

A highly significant secret agreement at Yalta, detailing the conditions under which Russia would enter the war against Japan, was
not made officially public until exactly a year later. The obvious reason
for secrecy was a desire not to provoke Japan until Hitler had been
disposed of and the Soviets could shift their troops to Siberia. Stalin
promised to enter the war "in two or three months" after the
surrender of Germany, but he demanded and secured a stiff price.
The *status quo* in Communist-dominated Outer Mongolia (once under
China's suzerainty) was to be preserved; the former rights of Russia,
lost in the Russo-Japanese War, were to be restored. These included
the return to Russia of the southern part of the island of Sakhalin;
the internationalization of the Manchurian port of Dairen (the pre-
eminent rights of Russia at this port to be safeguarded); and the
restoration to Russia of the lease of Port Arthur as a naval base.
Provision was also made for a joint operation of the Manchurian
railroads by both Chinese and Russians, with China retaining
sovereignty and the pre-eminent interests of the Soviet Union being
safeguarded. President Roosevelt undertook to persuade the Chinese
Nationalist government to accept these terms, some of which ran
directly counter to the pledges that he and Churchill had made to
Chiang Kai-shek at Cairo in 1943. In addition, Russia was to secure the
Japanese-owned Kurile Islands, which, American alarmists were
quick to note, might be used as bases for bombing the United States.

The terms of the secret agreement gradually leaked out, after both
Germany and Japan had been crushed, and when American confidence in Stalin's co-operativeness was evaporating. The Soviets, who
were adept at moving in once their boot was in the door, had
seemingly returned to Manchuria on essentially the same basis—in
some respects even stronger—than they had been when John Hay
had tried to jockey them out [in 1900]. The wheel had come full circle,
and as far as Manchuria was concerned the Open Door was completely unhinged.

The San Francisco Conference [to organize the United Nations], which met in the spring of 1945 with high hopes, marked a turning point in Soviet relations with the United States. Thereafter American public confidence in Stalin's willingness to co-operate in world organization began to spiral sharply downward.

The Moscow government, which revealed little interest in the new world league, chose a relatively obscure delegation. Only after a special appeal from the White House did Stalin consent to nominate Foreign Minister Molotov.

USSR at the UN

The Russian delegation, which arrived in San Francisco with a conspicuously strong bodyguard, created a disagreeable impression from the outset. Molotov championed the interests of the Soviet Union with belligerency. He insisted that the chairmanship of the Conference, instead of being held by the host nation (the United States), rotate among the Big Four. He urged representation for the new Polish government, which had been set up under Russian sponsorship. He vehemently but unsuccessfully demanded that "fascist" Argentina, which had not declared war on the Axis, be excluded from the Conference. He secured for the U.S.S.R., pursuant to the Yalta deal, three votes in the Assembly. He cavalierly brushed aside the rights of the small states, arguing that the big powers, which had borne the brunt of the fighting, should have the lion's share in running the postwar world. He vainly attempted to secure a veto over even discussion in the Security Council. He fought vigorously for the rights of colonial peoples, of whom the Soviet Union had none and of whom the leading Allied powers had many, notably Britain and France.

All this does not mean that there was not a large area of agreement between the Soviet Union and the United States at San Francisco, but the aggressive tactics of Molotov made sensational headlines. In many respects the small states, elbowing for a place, caused more of an uproar. The United States delegation, with an eye to approval by the Senate, was no less insistent than the Soviets on the general veto in the Security Council. But the net effect was to reinvigorate suspicions regarding Moscow which had been lulled by the war, and to implant doubts as to Russian co-operativeness in the future.

On August 8, 1945, three months to the day after the surrender of Germany, and in complete fulfillment of Stalin's pledge at Yalta, Russia declared war on Japan (effective August 9) and forthwith began to crush the emaciated Kwantung army in Manchuria. Six days later Japan surrendered and the Pacific war was over. By this narrow margin the Soviet Union almost failed to purchase a ticket at the prospective peace conference with Japan. We now know that the Russians were aware of Japanese peace feelers, and that they had been advised of the atomic bomb. The epochal detonation at Hiroshima came only two days before the Soviet declaration of war.

For several years an influential body of Americans had been annoyed because the Russians would not enter the Pacific combat. When the Soviet-German conflict ended, many of these critics believed that Moscow should at once declare war. We did not fully appreciate the difficulties of transferring huge forces and supplies a distance of some 8,000 miles from the European front to eastern Siberia. Stalin no doubt could have attacked sooner, with less preparation and possibly less success, had he felt under extreme compulsion to do so. But he presumably was not loath to let the Americans weaken themselves by incurring some serious casualties in fighting the Japanese. When the U.S.S.R. finally declared war, there was general rejoicing in the United States. We were faced with an invasion of Japan, which might cost hundreds of thousands of lives, and Russia participation would presumably save American boys by pinning down troops in Manchuria and in shortening the struggle.

But when it quickly became evident that Japan, dazed by atomic bombs, probably would have surrendered without Soviet intervention, our bitterness over Stalin's nonparticipation gave way to dissatisfaction over his participation. This feeling of annoyance increased when we heard that our Slavic allies were taking complete credit at home for having knocked out Japan; what the Yankees had not been able to do in over three years the Russians had done in only six days. The dissatisfaction intensified when we finally learned that at Yalta we had paid a high price to bribe Stalin into a war from which he could not have been kept at any price. With the wisdom of hindsight a multitude of Americans, especially those of anti-New Deal persuasion, clamored that the slippery Stalin had sold the sickly Roosevelt, advised by the sickly Harry Hopkins, a gigantic gold brick.

But what was the situation in February, 1945, when the Big Three conferred on the Crimea? Germany was far from finished, as we were reminded by the recent and bloody breakthrough culminating in the Battle of the Bulge. Frightful additional casualties were expected in the assault on the Japanese homeland. Even when Japan was crushed, the self-sufficing Japanese Kwantung army in Manchuria could presumably carry on for years, and it would have to be mopped up by American boys, with further staggering losses. There was no assurance at the time of the Yalta Conference that the atomic bomb would work, or work as devastatingly as it did, or produce the effects that were produced.

Stalin was in a position to drive a hard bargain at Yalta—and he did. But the fact is that he retreated from his maximum demands, and set a formal limit, for whatever it might be worth, on his current designs in eastern Asia. His bargaining position would have been a good deal stronger if he had remained on the sidelines as the over-shadowing power in the Far East, while we exhausted ourselves hammering down the gates of Japan. But the American people, unaware of all these possibilities, developed a suspicion of Soviet gains at Yalta that augured ill for amity in the postwar years. . . .

Public opinion When the conflict crashed to a close in Europe, we still cherished a substantial reservoir of good will for the stout-hearted Russians, who had saved our skins while saving their own. If the Kremlin had chosen to conciliate rather than alienate us, we no doubt would have been willing to contribute generously in technicians, materials, and money to the rehabilitation of war-ravaged Russia.

But within a few months our worst fears were aroused, and the reservoir of good will cracked wide open. Numerous public opinion polls showed that before the summer of 1946, and even earlier in some cases, the American people had by strong or overwhelming majorities reached the following disquieting conclusions:

1. Russia could not be trusted to co-operate effectively in the new world organization.

2. The foreign policies of the Soviet Union could not meet with our approval.

3. The dominance of Russia over her satellite neighbors was prompted by aggressive rather than defensive designs.

4. The Soviet Union was not a peace-loving nation.

5. Another world holocaust was probable within twenty-five or so years.

6. Russia was most likely to start it.

7. A "get tough" policy was needed to halt the Soviets.[2]

A small but vocal minority of Americans, preponderantly isolation-ists, were complaining that we should never have entered World War

---

[2] Conclusions based on an analysis of all the national public opinion polls for these years, the skeletonized results of which appear in *Public Opinion Quarterly*.

II; that the U.S.S.R. could have squeezed through without us; and that an exhausted Russia was preferable to the Communist threat that now confronted us.

Just as the Japanese unified the United States by their electrifying attack on Pearl Harbor, so the Russians—less spectacularly but hardly less effectively—united the Americans against them by their crude and blustering tactics. The American people were in a mood to be lulled to sleep, and by arousing them to prospective dangers the Soviet leaders thwarted their own ostensible ends. Stalin and Molotov were the real fathers of the huge and costly postwar preparedness program in the United States, Possibly their long-range strategy was to bankrupt the bastion of capitalism and soften it up for world revolution.

The myth has somehow gained currency that, if Roosevelt had not been stricken in the hour of victory, co-operation between Russia and America would have been brought to the high level of which he had dreamed.

This view is held by many admirers of the late President, and is also voiced by Communists and other Soviet apologists, especially those who seek an excuse for deteriorating relations. But whatever the views of the Soviet spokesman, the Russian masses, knowing vaguely of Roosevelt's friendliness and openhanded generosity with lend-lease largesse, held—and perhaps still hold—their benefactor in considerable esteem.

The proof is convincing—as detailed in the published postwar revelations of James F. Byrnes, Henry L. Stimson, and Harry L. Hopkins—that Roosevelt died knowing or strongly suspecting that his bold bid for conciliation had failed. The sharp shift in Soviet policy was clearly discernible by mid-March, 1945, about two weeks before the enfeebled and disillusioned President made his final trip to Warm Springs.

In March, 1945, the western Allies were negotiating for the surrender of the German army in Italy. Stalin, evidently fearing that certain German divisions would be released for action against the Red army, dispatched a scorching telegram to Roosevelt, reflecting on American truthfulness and good faith. Although the affair was finally patched up, the President was deeply hurt by the man whom he had familiarly called "Uncle Joe."

Roosevelt himself sent a sharp telegram to Stalin when he learned that the Russians were releasing captured American prisoners in out-of-the-way places, contrary to the Yalta agreement. We assumed, whether correctly or not, that the Soviet rulers did not want our officers to see their Communist infiltration in Poland and elsewhere.

Roosevelt likewise found the voracious designs of the Soviet-backed Yugoslavs on Italy's Trieste "wholly unjustified and deeply disquieting"—to quote Secretary Stimson.

By mid-March, 1945, the Soviets were clearly taking over Romania in violation of Stalin's pledges at Yalta.

Most distressing of all was unmistakable evidence that the Soviets, also in defiance of the Yalta pact, were setting up in Poland a prefabricated Communist government. Unless there was a freely constituted Polish regime, the heart would be cut out of the Yalta agreement, which would then turn out to be a cruel hoax.

On April 1, 1945, Roosevelt dispatched a vigorous telegram to Stalin remonstrating against Soviet usurpations in both Romania and Poland. The response being unsatisfactory, the President instructed the State Department to prepare a reply jointly with the British Foreign Office. Before the message could be sent he died, weary and sick at heart.

Why did the Kremlin so rudely slap aside the proffered hand of co-operation and fellowship?

The Soviets had never allied themselves with the western democracies in spirit, and when the fighting stopped there was a natural tendency for the Russian mind to return to—or remain in—the old grooves of antiwestern distrust. Secretary Hull concluded that Moscow started to launch out on its independent course as early as 1944, when it scented final victory and felt less dependent upon the democracies for aid. About the same time, and presumably for the same reason, Soviet spokesmen began to stress once more the orthodox Communist ideals of internationalism and world revolution, quite in contrast to their emphasis on nationalism during the wartime crisis.

This disquieting development was entirely natural. Communism, which openly proclaims warfare on capitalism, could not trust the democratic world, and Moscow's policy was no doubt permeated by anticapitalistic fears. Soviet misgivings were further fed by the irresponsible utterances of certain American newspapers and political leaders, including the prominent American legislator in Italy who in 1945 asked a group of American soldiers if they did not want to keep going right on to Moscow. The cloistered occupants of the Kremlin, having risen to precarious power with the cry of capitalistic encirclement, would be less indispensable and hence less secure if that encirclement should end. To co-operate would kill a substantial part of their reason for existence. Not only was it to their personal advantage to harp on western aggression, whether they really feared it or not, but an outside bogey would prove useful in quieting disunity at home and in arousing an already exhausted people to greater sacrifices.

The Soviet leaders at first were inclined to belittle the atomic bomb, but gradually they began to promote a fear psychosis among their people. Rich and powerful Uncle Sam had this horrible new weapon, loaded and ticking, and the Russians did not have it in 1945, and did not get it, according to our information, until four years later. The alarm of large segments of the Russian people over the so-called "rattling of the atom bomb" was unquestionably real, especially when no less a figure than ex-Governor George H. Earle of Pennsylvania, among others, could proclaim in 1946 that we should attack the Russians with the bomb "while we have it and before they get it."

To Americans, Soviet charges of aggression seemed ludicrous. With unprecedented haste and with a juvenile disregard of power realities, we had disbanded the fresh and potent mechanized army that had cracked Hitler's famed west wall. As for the atom bomb, Governor Earle's fulminations represented the views of an inconsequential minority. All we wanted was peace and a return to pre-war days.

Soviet fears of capitalistic aggression were further deepened by our attitude toward Moscow's dealings with its weaker neighbors, notably Poland, whose democratic status had presumably been guaranteed at Yalta. The protests of the western Allies against Soviet encroachments merely confirmed the Kremlin's suspicions, and provided the Russians with justification for building up anti-capitalistic puppets in neighboring countries before the democracies could foster anti-Communist regimes.

The leaders of Communist Russia harbored additional grievances. They professed to be angered by our open support of "fascist" Argentina at the San Francisco Conference. They were disconcerted by our abrupt and seemingly brutal termination of lend-lease, even though our cancellation was dictated by the terms of the law, and even though we continued for nearly two years to fulfill many of our commitments. They were angered by our vigorous support of France for a place on the reparations commission—a France that had left its allies in the lurch by hoisting the white flag of surrender five years before the end of the war. They were affronted by our inept handling of their request for a huge loan, which the State Department announced in 1946 had been "misplaced." But by this time so many things had gone wrong that American opinion, as nation-wide polls revealed, would not have tolerated substantial grants to rebuild the nation that was looming up as our most formidable potential foe.

The war-hating Americans were especially disturbed by the inability of the Soviet Union to agree with the western world on terms of peace for the fallen Axis foe. A series of meetings of the foreign ministers of the major powers, after prolonged wrangling, resulted by late 1946 in the drawing up of treaties for Hungary, Italy, Romania, Bulgaria, and Finland. But no agreement could be reached on Germany, Austria, or Japan.

The Austrian problem was peculiarly vexatious. We regarded the Austrians as a people liberated from the shackles of Hitler; the Soviets regarded them as willing accomplices of Hitler. We labored to protect Austrian assets and to rehabilitate an independent government. The Russians made off with assets for much-needed reparations, and undertook to thwart our efforts to create a democratically based regime. They also succeeded in defeating all our efforts to extend American principles of free navigation to the Danube. Painful clashes between tommy-gun-equipped Soviet soldiers and Americans added to the tension, as was true also in Berlin.

The prospect seemed even darker in Germany, which had been chopped up into four zones under the administration of Russia, Britain, France, and the United States respectively. Contrary to the Potsdam agreement of 1945, the Soviets seized reparations from current production; supported the temporary western boundary of Poland as a finality; blocked Allied efforts to treat Germany as an economic entity; and sought to communize Germany by propaganda, by the discriminatory distribution of food, and by other police-state methods. The Russians also retained hundreds of thousands of German prisoners of war, contrary to agreement, and deported or lured away German technicians, thus securing the know-how for making the latest-type submarines and other lethal weapons. (The United States by less arbitrary methods did substantially the same thing when it could.) The Soviets further opposed urgently needed currency reform, hounded displaced persons who had anti-Communist leanings, and, while seeking a hand in the joint control of the Ruhr, loudly accused the western powers of trying to revive Hitlerian cartels.

Secretaries of State Byrnes and Marshall, departing sharply from American tradition, vainly attempted to obtain Russian adherence to a twenty-five to forty-year treaty designed to keep Germany disarmed. The very fact that public opinion in the United States did not flare up violently against this forsaking of sacred principles is in itself eloquent testimony to the growing fear of the Soviet Union. The deadlock finally became so paralyzing that the three western Allies—Britain, France, and the United States—had no alternatives but to abandon their respective zones, leaving Germany with its enormous war potential to fall into the hands of Communist Russia, or to create an amputated new Germany around the three western zones. Following Secretary Byrnes' uncompromising speech at Stuttgart, Germany (September, 1946), serving notice that we were there to stay, determined steps were taken in the direction of establishing a western Germany, to the accompaniment of charges from Moscow that the Allies had broken the Potsdam pact. The ghost of Hitler must have laughed ghoulishly to see the democratic west building up Germany against Communist Russia.

The disheartening conviction gradually deepened among our citizenry that the Kremlin did not want agreement—except on its own terms. Delay and deadlock would produce further chaos in western Europe; and chaos is the natural seedbed of communism. When people become desperate enough, they will try almost anything. Starvation knows no ideology. Nor were the Soviet officials enthusiastic about reviving the German standard of living. The inhabitants of adjoining Communist countries might ask dangerous questions if their capitalistic neighbors enjoyed more consumers' goods, superior sanitary facilities, and other modern conveniences. Common misery would make for more willing Communists.

The Soviets of course had their own point of view regarding the four-power revival of central Europe. Their constant complaint— and one seemingly justified by events—was that the western bloc was trying to outvote them in conference and thus promote capitalism. They were right, in the sense that any rebuilding of Germany and Austria on pre-Hitlerian lines was antipathetic to communism.

2   FROM   *Gar Alperovitz*
            How Did the Cold War Begin?

In his interpretation of the Cold War's origins, Professor Bailey emphasized that the Soviet Union was the aggressor nation. Gar Alperovitz takes sharp issue with this view in the following selection. He constructs his argument around a review of Martin F. Herz's Beginnings of the Cold War *(Bloomington, Indiana, 1966). A Fellow at the Kennedy Institute at Harvard, Mr. Alperovitz was the author of a detailed and much discussed analysis of policy making in 1945,* Atomic Diplomacy: Hiroshima and Potsdam *(New York, 1965). Note particularly Mr. Alperovitz's interpretation of Franklin D. Roosevelt's implicit acceptance of Russian power in Eastern Europe and his view of Germany as the crucial issue in the Cold War. Is there an important change in American policy after the death of President Roosevelt? Which events are emphasized by Mr. Alperovitz, and how does his list of subjects differ from the events chosen for discussion by Professor Bailey?*

Writing as "Mr. X," George Kennan suggested twenty years ago that the mechanism of Soviet diplomacy "moves inexorably along the prescribed path, like a persistent toy automobile wound up and headed in a given direction, stopping only when it meets with some unanswerable force."[1] A generation of Americans quickly embraced Kennan's view as an explanation of the tension, danger, and waste of the Cold War. But was his theory of inexorable Soviet expansion— and its matching recommendation of "containment"—correct? A cautious but important book, *Beginnings of the Cold War*, suggests we might well have been more critical of so mechanistic an idea of the way Great Powers act and how the Cold War began.

Martin F. Herz is currently a United States diplomat serving in Teheran. His book is mainly concerned with the few months betweeen the 1945 Yalta and Potsdam Conferences. It is well-documented and contains no polemic; indeed, as he says, "the author expresses few views of his own. . . ." The book begins by recapitulating the main issues in dispute when Truman became President: Poland,

SOURCE. *New York Review of Books,* **VIII** (March 23, 1967), pp. 6–12. Reprinted by permission. This essay also appears in Gar Alperovitz, *Cold War Essays* (New York: Doubleday & Co., Inc., 1970).

[1] *Foreign Affairs,* July, 1947.

German reparations, lend-lease aid. It moves from the Polish issue to a broader discussion of spheres of influence, and from reparations and lend-lease to a general analysis of aid to Russia and its relation to other diplomatic considerations. The two issues are integrated in a brief concluding discussion of how the "die was cast" in 1945, and the Cold War began.

Any examination of the very earliest postwar period forces us to think about developments *before* 1947 when it was decided to contain the Soviet Union by "unanswerable force." Herz's study is important because it makes two serious judgments about this period: first, that in 1945 Soviet policy was by no means inexorably prescribed and expansionist; second, that mistakes made by American officials just after the war may well have prevented the kind of compromise and accommodation which is just beginning to emerge in Europe today. . . .

No one, of course, can be certain of "what might have been." But Herz refutes at least one accepted myth. Contrary to current historical reconstructions, there is abundant evidence that American leaders in 1945 were not much worried about the expansion of communism into *Western* Europe. That worry came later. In the days just after the war, most Communists in Italy, France, and elsewhere were cooperating with bourgeois governments. At Potsdam, in 1945, Truman regarded the Russian's desires for concessions beyond their area of occupation as largely bluff. The major issues in dispute were all in Eastern Europe, deep within the zone of Soviet military occupation. The real expansion of Soviet power, we are reminded, took place in Poland, Hungary, Bulgaria, Rumania, Czechoslovakia, and the eastern regions of Germany and Austria.

The U.S. in 1945 wanted Russia to give up the control and influence the Red Army had gained in the battle against Hitler. American demands may have been motivated by an idealistic desire to foster democracy, but Herz's main point is that in countries like Rumania and Bulgaria they were about as realistic as would be Soviet demands for changes in, say, Mexico. Any such parallel has obvious limits, the most significant of which is not that democracy and communism cannot so easily be compared, but that Eastern Europe is of far greater importance to Soviet security than is Mexico to American security: from the time of Napoleon—and twice in the lifetime of millions of presentday Russians—bloody invasions have swept through the area to their "Middle West."

In the early Spring of 1945, negotiations concerning one border state—Poland—brought the main issue into the open. At Yalta and immediately thereafter, the U.S. had mainly mediated between Stalin and Churchill on Poland; Roosevelt had warned Churchill that to make extreme demands would doom the negotiations. A month later, in the faltering last days of Roosevelt's life, the U.S. itself adopted a new tough line, demanding that pro-Western and openly anti-Russian Polish politicians be given more influence in negotiations to set up a new government for Poland. As was predicted, the Russians balked at the idea of such an expansion of anti-Soviet influence in a country so important to their security, and the negotiations ground to a halt. Moreover, at this precise moment, Russian suspicions about the West deepened with Allen Dulles's concurrent but unrelated secret negotiations with Nazi generals in Switzerland. The result was a violent quarrel which shook the entire structure of American-Soviet relations. But this was only the beginning. The demands on the Polish question reflected the ideas of the men who were to surround the new President; led by Joseph Grew and James F. Byrnes, they soon convinced Truman to attempt to make stronger demands elsewhere in Eastern Europe.

For most of the year Roosevelt had been highly ambivalent toward such matters. By late 1944, however, (in spite of wavering on the politically sensitive Polish issue in his dying days) Roosevelt concluded it would be a fundamental error to put too much pressure on Russia over other regions vital to her security. In September and October 1944, and early January 1945, he gave form to his conclusion by entering into armistice agreements with Britain and Russia, which gave the Soviet military almost complete control of internal politics in each Eastern European ex-Nazi satellite. It was understood, for instance, that the Soviets would have authority to issue orders to the Rumanian government, and that, specifically, the allied Control Commission would be "under the general direction of the Allied (Soviet) High Command acting on behalf of the Allied Powers." The Rumanian accords, and the similar but slightly less severe Bulgarian and Hungarian armistice agreements, served to formalize the famous Churchill-Stalin spheres-of-influence arrangement which, without F.D.R.'s agreement, had previously given the Russians "90 per cent" influence in Rumania, "80 per cent" influence in Bulgaria, and "75 per cent" influence in Hungary, in exchange for "90 per cent" British influence in Greece and a "50–50" split of influence in Yugoslavia. The armistice accords were also modeled after a previous understanding which had contained Soviet endorsement of dominant American-British influence in Italy. The Eastern European armistice agreements have been available to the public for years, but have been successfully buried, or avoided by most scholars. Herz has exhumed them, and he shows that they contain American endorsement of dominant Soviet influence in the ex-Nazi satellites.

At Yalta, in early February, 1945, Roosevelt pasted over these specific texts the vague and idealistic rhetoric of the famous Declaration on Liberated Europe. The President apparently wished to use the Declaration mainly to appease certain politically important ethnic groups in America; he devoted only a few minutes to the matter at the Yalta Conference, and the familiar rhetoric promising democracy was almost devoid of practical meaning. For example, who was to decide in given instances between the American and Soviet definitions of common but vague terms like "democratic"? Much more important, as Herz shows, in the broad language of the Declaration the Allies agreed merely to "consult" about matters within the liberated countries, not to "act," and they authorized consultations only when all parties agreed they were necessary. Thus the United States itself confirmed the Russians' right to refuse to talk about the ex-Nazi satellites. The State Department knew this and, in fact, had tried to insert operative clauses into the Declaration. But Roosevelt, having just signed the armistice agreements, rejected this unrealistic proposal. Moreover, when the Soviets after Yalta crudely tossed out a Rumanian government they did not like, the President, though unhappy that he had not been consulted, reaffirmed his basic position by refusing to intervene.

Ironically, Herz's book lends credence to the old Republican charge that Roosevelt accepted a compromise at Yalta which bolstered Stalin's position in Eastern Europe. The charge, while correct in essentials, was silly in assuming that much else, short of war, could have been done while the Red Army occupied the area. The Republican politicians also ignored the fact that at Yalta Roosevelt could not expect a continued American military presence in Europe for very long after the war. This not only deprived him of leverage, it made an accommodation with Russia much more desirable for another reason: Red Army help became essential as a guarantee that Germany would not rise from defeat to start yet a third World War. Stalin also needed American help, as he too made clear, to hold down the Germans. Hence, underlying the American-Soviet plans for peace at Yalta was not "faith" but a common interest—the German threat—which had cemented the World War II alliance. From this 1945 perspective the crucial portion of the Yalta agreement was not the Declaration on Liberated Europe, nor even the provisions on Poland, but rather the understanding that the United States and Russia (with Britain and France as minor partners) would work together to control Germany. This meant, among other things, joint action to reduce Germany's physical power by extracting reparations from German industry.

Although Herz tends to play down the German issue, he does take up important economic matters that relate to it. He understands that Moscow was in a cruel dilemma which, had the U.S. been shrewd enough, might have been resolved to the benefit of both American diplomacy and the economic health of Europe. The Russians were greatly in need of aid for their huge postwar reconstruction program. Importing industrial equipment from Eastern Europe was a possible solution, though a doubtful one, for taking this equipment would inevitably cause political problems. Reparations from Germany were another, but the key industrial sectors were in American hands. Finally, the United States itself was a potential source. Herz argues (as did Ambassadors Harriman and Winant at the time) that a U.S. reconstruction loan for Russia would have been wise; it would have given U.S. diplomacy strong leverage in a variety of negotiations. (Without other sources of aid for reconstruction the Russians were almost inevitably reduced to extracting industrial goods from either Germany or Eastern Europe.) American officials seriously considered such a loan, but, as Herz shows, they did not actively pursue it with the Russians—though one or two crude attempts were made to use a loan as a bludgeon in negotiations. With a future U.S. troop commitment unlikely, and a large loan ruled out, the United States had no real bargaining power. Hence its attempts at intervention in Eastern Europe amounted to little more than bluster.

The State Department wanted to have it both ways: it wanted to hold the Russians to the vague promises of the Yalta Declaration; it also wanted to avoid the specific texts of the armistice agreements. But the Republicans, and even Secretary Byrnes in his later writings, understood the weakness of this position. The Republicans, for their part, also wanted to have it both ways. They wanted to argue both that Roosevelt gave the Russians all the authority they needed for their actions *and* that the Russians broke their agreements.

The Republican attack on Yalta came late in the Cold War, and was combined with a new demand that the U.S. "roll back" Soviet influence. Few now realize how unoriginal the demand was, for a "roll back" effort—without its latter-day label—was, in fact, at the center of Harry Truman's first postwar policy. The President, we now know, made this effort in a spurt of confidence derived from the new atomic bomb. But the policy failed in its continuing attempt to reduce Soviet control by expanding Western influence in Poland. It also failed in its bold follow-up effort to force the Russians to change the Bulgarian and Rumanian government. Nevertheless, these opening moves of the postwar period helped to set the tone of the new Administration's attitude toward Russia. Truman, although publicly proclaiming his adherence to Roosevelt's policy of cooperation, seems to have understood that his approach differed fundamentally from his predecessor's. (In private, as Secretary of State Stettinius has written, he complained that the intervention in Poland rested on rather shaky diplomatic ground.) Indeed, by September 1945, the basic change in U.S. policy was so clearly defined that, as Secretary of State Byrnes later wrote, the Russian complaint that Roosevelt's policy had been abandoned was "understandable."[2]

What was the result? Like Herz, John Foster Dulles (who assisted Byrnes at the time) also believed that the Cold War began in 1945. Dulles emphasized in his book *War or Peace* (1950) that a new tough line of U.S. policy was adopted at this time over dimly remembered issues deep within the Soviet-controlled Balkans. Herz prints almost the full text of the crucial 1945 Hopkins-Stalin talks, which reveal the equally important point that, in Russia, the change in American policy produced what Stalin termed "a certain alarm." A few thoughtful U.S. officials recognized the significance of these developments. Secretary of War Henry L. Stimson, for example, tried to block the campaign to engage American prestige in Eastern Europe. In White House discussions he argued, first, that the demand for more Western influence in Poland was a mistake: "The Russians perhaps were being more realistic than we were in regard to their own security. . . ." He then tried to cut short efforts to intervene elsewhere, reminding Truman, as Stimson's diary shows, that "we have made up our minds on the broad policy that it was not wise to get into the Balkan mess even if the thing seemed to be disruptive of policies which the State Department thought were wise." Stimson pointed out that "we have taken that policy right from the beginning, Mr. Roosevelt having done it himself or having been a party to it himself."

[2] *Speaking Frankly*, Harper, 1947.

When Stimson failed in his conservative effort to limit American objectives, the stage was set for one of the great tragedies of the Cold War. As Stimson understood, the Russians, though extremely touchy about the buffer area, were not impossible to deal with. Had their security requirements been met, there is evidence that their domination of Eastern Europe might have been much different from what it turned out to be. Churchill, too, thought the Russians were approachable. Obviously, conditions in Eastern Europe would not meet Western ideals; but Churchill judged, in late 1944 and early 1945, that Moscow was convinced it would be much easier to secure its objectives through moderate policies. In Greece at this time, as Churchill was to stress in *Triumph and Tragedy*, Stalin was "strictly and faithfully" holding to his agreement *not* to aid the Greek Communists. Even in much of the border area the Russians seemed willing to accept substantial capitalism and some form of democracy —with the crucial proviso that the Eastern European governments had to be "friendly" to Russia in defense and foreign policies. Finland serves as a rough model of a successful border state. Here, too, the armistice made the Soviets supreme, giving rights parallel to the Bulgarian and Rumanian accords plus the right to maintain Soviet military installations. However, the U.S. made no independent effort to intervene; Finland maintained a foreign policy "friendly" to Russia; and the Russians were—as they still seem to be—prepared to accept a moderate government.

Although it is often forgotten, a modified application of the Finnish formula seemed to be shaping up elsewhere in 1945 and much of 1946. In Hungary, Soviet-sponsored free elections routed the Communist Party in 1945. In Bulgaria, a country with rather weak democratic traditions, the 1945 elections were complicated by competition for Great Power support among the various internal factions. Certainly the results were not perfect, but most Western observers (except the State Department) felt they should have been accepted. In Austria, the Communists were swamped in Soviet-run free elections in their zone in 1945, and, after a hesitant start, a free democratic government emerged for the entire country. In Czechoslovakia, from which the Red Army withdrew in December of 1945, democracy was so clearly acceptable to Soviet policy that the U.S. had little to protest at the time.

Almost all of this was to change, of course. The freedoms in Hungary were to end in 1947. The initial pattern in Czechoslovakia was to be reversed in 1948. But writers who focus only on the brutal period of totalitarian control after 1947 and 1948 often ignore what happened earlier. The few who try to account for the known facts of the 1945–1946 interlude usually do so in passing, either to suggest that the democratic governments "must have been" mere smoke-screens formed while Moscow waited for the U.S. to leave the Continent; or that the Russians "must have been" secretly planning to take full control, but were methodically using the early period to prepare the groundwork for what came later. (Communists, too, like to ignore the 1945–1946 period, for it suggests the possibility that Soviet Russia was more interested in an old-fashioned *modus vivendi* with the capitalists than in spreading World Communism. This was the essence of Tito's bitter complaint that Stalin tried to turn back the Yugoslav revolution.)

The Russians have displayed so much duplicity, brutality, and intransigence that it is easy to imagine the 1945–1946 interlude as a mere smokescreen. But they also have a long history of protecting "socialism in one country" in a rather conservative, nationalistic way: the moderation of the 1945–1946 interlude can be viewed as a logical extension of this tradition. That at least two quite different interpretations of their 1945–1946 policy are conceivable is now rarely admitted, and the relative merits of each have not been seriously examined. Herz's study calls for a careful reappraisal of early postwar Soviet objectives. If the Russians were secretly harboring plans for an ultimate take over, they certainly were preparing a lot of trouble for themselves by sponsoring free politics, by pulling out the Red Army (it is not particularly shrewd to have to *re*-introduce foreign troops), by ripping up the Red Army's main rail connections across Poland—as they did in the fall of 1945. As well informed an observer as Averell Harriman believed, as he once testified to Congress, that Soviet policy in 1945 was ambivalent, that it could have become either more moderate within a framework of security and understanding with the West, or that it could have become hard-line and totalitarian, within the framework of insecurity and conflict. Harriman, though puzzled by the ultimate Russian decision in favor of the iron-fisted policy, clearly saw that Soviet expansion was neither inexorable nor inevitable.

At least one reason for Russia's shift to a tough line may be traced to mistakes made by U.S. officials. As Stimson argued—and as history later showed—the demand for more influence in Soviet-controlled areas was almost certainly doomed from the start. This basic miscalculation stemmed, finally, from an attempt to overextend *American* diplomatic sway. Lippmann was, I believe correct in seeing that the other error was the failure of U.S. policy makers to turn their energies to an early solution of the crucial German problem. Bolstered by the atomic bomb, which eliminated the threat that had been Roosevelt's central concern, American leaders dallied over Germany. Moreover, by refusing to hold to Roosevelt's agreement that a specific target for German reparations would be set (July, 1945), by permitting France to hamstring the German Control Commission (Fall, 1945), by halting German reparations shipments (Spring, 1946)—U.S. policy suggested the very prospect Russia feared most: the abandonment of economic and political controls and the possibility that a new and powerful Germany would rise from the ashes of Nazism to become the bastion of Western capitalistic aggression in Europe. The United States had no such aggressive intent. Nonetheless, the U.S. chose not to negotiate seriously on Germany until a full year-and-a-half after the war's end. Especially after Secretary Byrnes's tough speech in Stuttgart in the Fall of 1946, American policy was shortsighted enough to suggest a threat to Russia at the very time it was attempting to weaken Soviet control in the vital area which lay—protectively or threateningly—between German power and the Russian heartland. The Russians, who had no nuclear weapons, were far less casual about the question of security; their grip seemed to tighten in the buffer area month by month, as their worst fears about Germany seemed to come true.

The Russians were not easy to deal with, either in Germany or elsewhere. Nevertheless, if the hypothesis suggested by Lippmann's book is correct—and Herz's study indirectly supports it—there are reasons to believe that U.S. policy itself may have to share responsibility for the imposition of totalitarian control in Eastern Europe, and possibly also for the subsequent expanding Communist agitation in Western Europe. The *addition* of increased insecurity to known Soviet paranoid tendencies may explain the rigidity which Soviet leaders displayed in their satellite policy after 1946. The first pattern seemed crudely similar to the Finnish or Austrian models. Would it have been reversed had the U.S. seriously tried from the first to resolve the European security problem—as Lippmann urged? That Soviet actions may have been in part reactions to their judgments of American intentions may also help to explain why sustained Communist opposition developed in the West only *after* the clear breakdown of German control arrangements. It was not in 1945, but late in 1946 and in 1947 that the Italian and French Communists began to reverse their initial policy of cooperation with bourgeois governments. Was the changed focus of Communist politics part of the inexorable plan? Or was it primarily a rather shortsighted response to American policy itself?

Once the Communists became active in Western Europe, of course, the United States was faced with quite another set of issues. Disputes with Russia moved out of the border regions. The threat some officials had anticipated while reading Marx and listening to Communist propaganda began to become a political reality. In 1947, those who proposed a mechanical theory of Soviet expansion had to deal with expanding Communist political activity in the West. And it was in July of that year, precisely two years after Truman faced Stalin in his first Potsdam showdown over Eastern Europe, that Kennan's containment recommendation was publicly offered.

We do not yet have answers to all the questions about postwar American-Russian relations, but we know enough to consider afresh whether either of the Great Powers ever really did move inexorably, like a wound-up toy automobile, as "Mr. X" argued. Herz's sturdy little book suggests they did not, and is at least the beginning of a more subtle explanation of the complex sequence of interacting events which produced the Cold War.

CHAPTER II
MOTIVATIONS:
THE AMERICAN CENTURY
VERSUS BRITISH AND SOVIET
SPHERES

3 FROM   *Henry Luce and John Chamberlain*
        Must This Be the American Century? (1941)

Henry Luce, founder and Editor-in-Chief of Time *and* Life *magazines, published* The American Century *initially as an editorial in* Life *in early 1941, that is, before the United States entered the war. Luce nevertheless assumed that in reality Americans were already cobelligerents. His primary concern was to begin a discussion of post-war peace aims. Luce's essay had immense impact. It stressed topics, such as the sale of surplus industrial and agricultural goods, which were on the minds of all Americans who had suffered through the depression of the 1930s, and the analysis was presented in simple, stark terms. Equally appealing was the idealism ("We must undertake now to be the Good Samaritan of the entire world") with which he wrapped his argument. The implications of Luce's plan, however, were not as simple and appealing as the bare plan itself; these were spelled out by John Chamberlain, one of Luce's own editors in the* Time-Life *empire. Could Mr. Luce's view of American needs accept Mr. Chamberlain's declaration, "So instead of the 'American Century,' I would like to see a century in which people are left alone to pursue their own desires."?*

SOURCE. Henry R. Luce, *The American Century* (New York: Farrar & Rinehart, Inc., 1941), pp. 16–19, 23–25, 27, 29–30, 35–40, 68–71. Reprinted by permission of Time, Inc. (*Life* Magazine, February 17, 1941).

HENRY LUCE

Each of us stands ready to give our life, our wealth, and all our hope of personal happiness, to make sure that America shall not lose any war she is engaged in. But we would like to know what war we are trying to win—and what we are supposed to win when we win it. . . .

Furthermore—and this is an extraordinary and profoundly historical fact which deserves to be examined in detail—America and only America can effectively state the war aims of this war. . . .

We Americans no longer have the *alibi* that we cannot have things the way we want them so far as Great Britain is concerned. With due regard for the varying problems of the members of the British Commonwealth, what we want will be okay with them. . . .

America cannot be responsible for the good behavior of the entire world. But America is responsible to herself as well as to history, for the world-environment in which she lives. Nothing can so vitally affect America's environment as America's own influence upon it, and therefore if America's environment is unfavorable to the growth of American life, then America has nobody to blame so deeply as she must blame herself.

In its failure to grasp this relationship between America and America's environment lies the moral and practical bankruptcy of any and all forms of isolationism. It is most unfortunate that this virus of isolationist sterility has so deeply infected an influential section of the Republican Party. . . .

But politically speaking, it is an equally serious fact that for seven years Franklin Roosevelt was, for all practical purposes, a complete isolationist. He was more of an isolationist than Herbert Hoover or Calvin Coolidge. . . . There is of course a justification which can be made for the President's first two terms. It can be said, with reason, that great social reforms were necessary in order to bring democracy up-to-date in the greatest of democracies. But the fact is that Franklin Roosevelt failed to make American democracy work successfully on a narrow, materialistic and nationalistic basis. And under Franklin Roosevelt we ourselves have failed to make democracy work successfully. Our only chance now to make it work is in terms of a vital international economy and in terms of an international moral order. . . .

Consider the 20th Century. It is ours not only in the sense that we happen to live in it but ours also because it is America's first century as a dominant power in the world. So far, this century of ours has been a profound and tragic disappointment. No other century has been so big with promise for human progress and happiness. And in no one century have so many men and women and children suffered such pain and anguish and bitter death. . . .

Any true conception of our world of the 20th Century must surely include a vivid awareness of at least these four propositions.

First: our world of 2,000,000,000 human beings is for the first time in history one world, fundamentally indivisible. Second: modern man hates war and feels intuitively that, in its present scale and frequency, it may even be fatal to his species. Third: our world, again for the first time in human history, is capable of producing all the material needs of the entire human family. Fourth: the world of the 20th Century, if it is to come to life in any nobility of health and vigor, must be to a significant degree an American Century. . . .

Consider four areas of life and thought in which we may seek to realize such a vision:

First, the economic. It is for America and for America alone to determine whether a system of free economic enterprise—an economic order compatible with freedom and progress—shall or shall not prevail in this century. We know perfectly well that there is not the slightest chance of anything faintly resembling a free economic system prevailing in this country if it prevails nowhere else. What then does America have to decide? Some few decisions are quite simple. For example: we have to decide whether or not we shall have for ourselves and our friends freedom of the seas—the right to go with our ships and our ocean-going airplanes where we wish, when we wish and as we wish. The vision of America as the principal guarantor of the freedom of the seas, the vision of America as the dynamic leader of world trade, has within it the possibilities of such enormous human progress as to stagger the imagination. Let us not be staggered by it. Let us rise to its tremendous possibilities. Our thinking of world trade today is on ridiculously small terms. For example, we think of Asia as being worth only a few hundred millions a year to us. Actually, in the decades to come Asia will be worth to us exactly zero—or else it will be worth to us four, five, ten billions of dollars a year. And the latter are the terms we must think in, or else confess a pitiful impotence.

Closely akin to the purely economic area and yet quite different from it, there is the picture of an America which will send out through the world its technical and artistic skills. Engineers, scientists, doctors, movie men, makers of entertainment, developers of air-lines, builders of roads, teachers, educators. . . .

But now there is a third thing which our vision must immediately be concerned with. We must undertake now to be the Good Samaritan of the entire world. It is the manifest duty of this country to under-take to feed all the people of the world who as a result of this world-wide collapse of civilization are hungry and destitute—all of them, that is, whom we can from time to time reach consistently with a very tough attitude toward all hostile governments. For every dollar we spend on armaments, we should spend at least a dime in a gigantic effort to feed the world—and all the world should know that we have dedicated ourselves to this task. Every farmer in America should be encouraged to produce all the crops he can, and all that we can-not eat—and perhaps some of us could eat less—should forthwith be dispatched to the four quarters of the globe as a free gift, administered by a humanitarian army of Americans, to every man, woman and child on this earth who is really hungry.

But all this is not enough. All this will fail and none of it will happen unless our vision of America as a world power includes a passionate devotion to great American ideals. We have some things in this country which are infinitely precious and especially American—a love of freedom, a feeling for the equality of opportunity, a tradi-tion of self-reliance and independence and also of co-operation. In addition to ideals and notions which are especially American, we are the inheritors of all the great principles of Western civilization—above all Justice, the love of Truth, the ideal of Charity. The other day Herbert Hoover said that America was fast becoming the sanc-tuary of the ideals of civilization. For the moment it may be enough to be the sanctuary of these ideals. But not for long. It now becomes our time to be the powerhouse from which the ideals spread through-out the world and do their mysterious work of lifting the life of man-kind from the level of the beasts to what the Psalmist called a little lower than the angels. . . .

It is in this spirit that all of us are called, each to his own measure of capacity, and each in the widest horizon of his vision, to create the first great American Century.

JOHN CHAMBERLAIN

. . . Mr. Luce's program requires a faith that can only be sustained for short periods, when people are in the heroic mood. Mr. Luce believes in what might be called straight-line Prometheanism; I believe that people are less heroic, and thank God that they are. (If they weren't rather ordinary in a nice humdrum sort of way they would be killing each other in the name of noble philosophies all the time instead of once every twenty or thirty years.) And since people aren't normally Promethean in large numbers, Mr. Luce's program must, in ordinary times, fall into the hands of the hypocrites who are skilled in using the great slogans to hail nefarious purposes. If we must fight in the near future, I would prefer to see us fight for limited aims—say for the purely practical purpose of keeping England from being run over. No large, glittering commitments, no guarantees that Europe and the world must be thus and so forever. In the first place, we aren't up to implementing the guarantees; in the second place, no one likes paternalism, the supervision of the "do-gooder," for very long. In times of trouble the Filipinos and the Puerto Ricans and the followers of Gandhi tend to forget their "nationalism." But when peace comes? Ah, on *that* day they want to run themselves, even if it involves the democratic risk of running themselves into the ground. Just now China needs help in fighting Japan. But if she drives the Japanese out she will not want to be coerced by the subtle or not-so-subtle suggestions of foreign bankers, private or governmental, from the United States or Britain; her own growing middle class will want to take charge of China's productive machine for themselves. If Mr. Luce were in charge of loans to China I would trust him to relinquish control at the proper time. But Mr. Luce *isn't* the banker, and I'm not writing psychological blank checks for people I've never seen.

So instead of the "American Century," I would like to see a century in which people are left alone to pursue their own desires. This does not mean that every little Latvia or Rumania must be restored, or that every small war of neighborhood conquest must be "prevented" (i.e., turned into a world war). It does mean that *large* powers (the workable machine-age units) should learn to live at peace with other *large* powers, lest every border scuffle or need for regional integration become Armageddon once more. . . . As for future economics, it means that when peace comes the United States should turn to developing its home market, not in the autarchic sense, but for the simple reason that when Detroit and Akron and Camden, New Jersey, are prosperous we buy rubber and tin and other things from the outside world in sufficient quantities to give foreigners the dollar exchange that is needed before they can buy from us.

Phil LaFollette [Governor of Wisconsin] once said the present crisis could be surmounted in one of two ways: the German way or the Swedish way. I believe he is right, or will be proved right in the long run. . . . And of this I am sure: that if the United States does not accept the Swedish way of solving her problems, she must turn to an imperialism that will fail in liberality and become something very close to the Nazi thing. I can't prove this within the present spatial limitations: but I invite readers to think it over for themselves when giving content to the high-order abstraction that is the "American Century."

4   FROM   *The Atlantic Charter*

Roosevelt and Churchill Announce the Principles
for the Postwar World (August 14, 1941.)

Although Henry Luce criticized Franklin D. Roosevelt's policies in The American Century, *the American President was following a line of thought in regard to post-war peace objectives which was similar to Mr. Luce's. The most dramatic presentation of these aims was the Atlantic Charter, written by President Roosevelt and British Prime Minister Winston Churchill at a highly secret meeting held August 9–12, 1941 on board a warship off Argentia, Newfoundland. In certain respects, Luce had outlined the objectives, and the Atlantic Charter discussed the tactics. The Charter was only one result of the Argentia conference. The President also acknowledged the increased American involvement in the war by warning Japan not to attack the Pacific holdings of England and Holland, and he promised American naval convoys for British cargo ships moving between the British Isles and Iceland. As Luce had assumed, the United States was becoming an actual partner of the British in the war against Hitler, although Pearl Harbor was still nearly four months away. Post-war planning nevertheless already occupied the President's mind. In what particulars might the Charter have been different if the Soviet Union (which by mid-August had been fighting the Nazis for nearly two months) had attended the conference?*

Joint declaration of the President of the United States of America and the Prime Minister, Mr. Churchill, representing His Majesty's

SOURCE. U.S. Department of State, *Foreign Relations of the United States, 1941*, I, pp. 366–368 (Washington, D.C.: 1958).

Government in the United Kingdom, being met together, deem it right to make known certain common principles in the national policies of their respective countries on which they base their hopes for a better future for the world.

First, their countries seek no aggrandizement, territorial or other;

Second, they desire to see no territorial changes that do not accord with the freely expressed wishes to the peoples concerned;

Third, they respect the right of all peoples to choose the form of government under which they will live; and they wish to see sovereign rights and self government restored to those who have been forcibly deprived of them;

Fourth, they will endeavor, with due respect for their existing obligations, to further the enjoyment by all States, great or small, victor or vanquished, of access, on equal terms, to the trade and to the raw materials of the world which are needed for their economic prosperity;

Fifth, they desire to bring about the fullest collaboration between all nations in the economic field with the object of securing, for all, improved labor standards, economic advancement, and social security;

Sixth, after the final destruction of the Nazi tyranny, they hope to see established a peace which will afford to all nations the means of dwelling in safety within their own boundaries, and which will afford assurance that all men in all the lands may live out their lives in freedom from fear and want;

Seventh, such a peace should enable all men to traverse the high seas and oceans without hindrance;

Eighth, they believe that all of the nations of the world, for realistic as well as spiritual reasons must come to the abandonment of the use of force. Since no future peace can be maintained if land, sea or air armaments continue to be employed by nations which threaten, or may threaten, aggression outside of their frontiers, they believe, pending the establishment of a wider and permanent system of general security, that the disarmament of such nations is essential. They will likewise aid and encourage all other practicable measures which will lighten for peace-loving peoples the crushing burden of armaments.

5   FROM   *British and Soviets Attach*
               Limitations to the Atlantic Charter
                      (September 1941)

Several principles of the Atlantic Charter could be interpreted as attacks on long-established British policies. The third article (respecting "the right of all peoples to choose the form of government under which they will live") could be viewed as a promise that India and other parts of the British Empire would soon be given complete independence. The fourth article (promising "access, on equal terms, to the trade and to the raw materials of the world") could be seen as an attack against the British Imperial Preference System, established in the early 1930s to give Great Britain and her Commonwealth special trading privileges not granted to those outside the Commonwealth, such as the United States. On his return to England, Prime Minister Churchill explained to Parliament his interpretation of the Charter. Later in September 1941, the Russians were asked to sign the Charter. They did so, but only after adding a significant reservation which, in Stalin's mind, must have related to two areas: the Baltic states, which the Soviets occupied and essentially reannexed to their empire in 1940–1941; and areas in Eastern Europe, such as Poland and Czechoslovakia, through which German armies had passed twice in twenty-five years to attack Russia. At this point, the Soviets essentially excluded the Baltic states (Latvia, Lithuania, Estonia) and other areas of Eastern Europe from the Charter's principles. With the British and Soviet reservations, what remained of the Atlantic Charter?

THE PRIME MINISTER (MR. CHURCHILL), SPEAKING IN
COMMONS, SEPTEMBER 9, 1941

. . . First, the Joint Declaration does not try to explain how the broad principles proclaimed by it are to be applied to each and every case, which will have to be dealt with when the war comes to an end. It would not be wise for us, at this moment, to be drawn into laborious discussions on how it is to fit all the manifold problems with which we shall be faced after the war. Secondly, the Joint Declaration does not qualify in any way the various statements of policy which have been made from time to time about the development of constitutional

SOURCE. For British statement: *Parliamentary Debates, Fifth Series—Volume 374, House of Commons*, columns 68–69 of September 9, 1941; for Soviet reservation: *Report of Proceedings, Inter-Allied Meeting held in London at St. James Palace on September 24, 1941* (London: 1941).

government in India, Burma or other parts of the British Empire. We are pledged by the Declaration of August, 1940, to help India to obtain free and equal partnership in the British Commonwealth with ourselves, subject, of course, to the fulfillment of obligations arising from our long connection with India and our responsibilities to its many creeds, races and interests. . . . At the Atlantic meeting, we had in mind, primarily, the restoration of the sovereignty, self-government and national life of the States and nations of Europe now under the Nazi yoke, and the principles governing any alterations in the territorial boundaries which may have to be made. So that is quite a separate problem from the progressive evolution of self-governing institutions in the regions and peoples which owe allegiance to the British Crown. We have made declarations on these matters which are complete in themselves, free from ambiguity and related to the conditions and circumstances of the territories and peoples affected. They will be found to be entirely in harmony with the high conception of freedom and justice which inspired the Joint Declaration.

STATEMENT BY I. MAISKY, AMBASSADOR OF THE
SOVIET UNION TO GREAT BRITAIN, AS HE ACCEPTS THE
ATLANTIC CHARTER PRINCIPLES ON BEHALF OF THE
RUSSIAN GOVERNMENT (SEPTEMBER 24, 1941)

Considering that the practical application of these principles will necessarily adapt itself to the circumstances, needs, and historic peculiarities of particular countries, the Soviet Government can state that a consistent application of these principles will secure the most energetic support on the part of the government and peoples of the Soviet Union.

6 FROM   *Stalin-Eden Talks*
"It Now Looks as if the [Atlantic] Charter
was Directed Against the U.S.S.R."
(December 16–17, 1941).

*After the attack on Pearl Harbor, British Foreign Secretary Anthony Eden flew
to Moscow to discuss with Stalin common Anglo-American-Russian concerns. The
Soviet leader proceeded to spell out what had only been implied by the Russian
reservation to the Atlantic Charter on September 24. Stalin wanted to discuss
particulars (the Baltic States, the Polish boundary), and wanted the agreements
set down explicitly ("I do not wish to decry algebra, but I prefer practical arithmetic").
His attitude was particularly striking since German armies had moved over western
Russia very rapidly. Some observers did not believe that the Soviets would survive
the war, yet Stalin was boldly making specific demands for post-war Russian security.
Eden's responses were less than satisfactory to the Soviet dictator, in part because of
American reluctance to go beyond the Atlantic Charter principles in discussing the
post-war world. Washington officials, fearing that negotiating specific post-war boundaries would divide the Big Three and hinder the war effort, decided to delay making
any such commitments. As indicated in the following selection, Stalin was suspicious
of such delays. What are the geographical boundaries of Stalin's concerns? If these
concerns run counter to the Charter, which should receive priority, the Charter or
Stalin's view of the needs of Russian security?*

DECEMBER 16th

Read telegrams and worked in morning. Far Eastern situation looks
ugly. Russian and Libyan news good. Our first interview with Stalin
at 7 P.M. It continued until nearly 11 P.M. In the concluding stages
tea and cakes were brought in but nobody took much interest in them,
except Cripps [Sir Stafford Cripps, British Ambassador in Moscow].
After about half an hour's interval brandy followed with zakoushka
and champagne in which many toasts were drunk. All was friendly.
Stalin is a quiet dictator in his manner. No shouting, no gesticulation,
so that it is impossible to guess his meaning, or even the subject of
which he is speaking until the translation is given. Maisky [Ivan

SOURCE. Anthony Eden, Earl of Avon, *The Reckoning* (Boston: 1965), excerpts from
pp. 334–345. Reprinted by permission of Houghton Mifflin Company publishers.

Maisky, Soviet Ambassador to Great Britain] was a good inter-
preter. . . .

At first meeting Stalin gave me the drafts of two short treaties.
One was for a military alliance during the war, the other provided
for common action to solve post-war questions in Europe and to
prevent renewed aggression by Germany. Both these treaties were to
be published, but the second one was to have a secret protocol dealing
in some detail with European frontiers.

Stalin's suggestions for this protocol showed me that the hope we
had held in London, of being able to confine the discussion of
frontiers to the general terms of the Atlantic Charter, had been vain.
Russian ideas were already starkly definite. They changed little during
the next three years, for their purpose was to secure the most
tangible physical guarantees for Russia's future security.

Stalin proposed that Poland should expand westward at
Germany's expense. Other occupied countries were to return to
their old frontiers, Austria being restored, while the Rhineland
and possibly Bavaria would be detached from Germany. The Soviet
Union would regain her frontiers of 1941 with Finland and Roumania and would recover the Baltic States. Her frontier with Poland
would be based on the Curzon line. [The Curzon line, proposed by
the British at the Peace Conference of 1919–1920, was considerably
west of the actual Russo-Polish boundary between 1921 and 1939;
on the other hand, as a result of the Nazi-Soviet pact of
1939, the new Russo-Polish boundary moved west of the Curzon line
thereby giving Russia large portions of Poland.] Stalin also wanted
the right to establish bases in Finland and Roumania with a guarantee
for the exits from the Baltic. The Soviet Government would not
object, he said, to Britain establishing bases in Denmark and Norway.

Stalin then put two questions. What were our views about reparation by Germany for the damage she had done, and how were we to
keep peace and order in Europe after the war. He suggested a council
of the victorious powers, with a military force at its disposal. The
Soviet Union would have no objection if some European countries
wished to federate.

I told Stalin that I agreed with much that he had said about post-
war Europe. The British people were determined that every possible
military measure should be taken to prevent Germany breaking the
peace again. Exactly how this was to be done would have to be gone
into carefully. There was no doubt that some kind of military control
over Germany would be necessary and that Great Britain, the Soviet

Union, and the United States, if they would help, would have to undertake it.

On the partition of Germany, I said, the British government had not taken a decision either way. There was no objection to it in principle. Nor had we closed our minds to a separate Bavaria or Rhineland; we were certainly in favour of an independent Austria. . . . So far as reparations were concerned, I was sure, from our experience after the last war, that we should be against any money reparations; the restitution by Germany of goods taken away from occupied territories was another matter.

I then explained to Stalin that I could not agree to the secret protocol without reference to the Cabinet and added:

Even before Russia was attacked, Mr. Roosevelt sent a message to us, asking us not to enter into any secret arrangement as to the post-war reorganization of Europe without first consulting him. This does not exclude our two countries from discussing a basis for the peace. . . .

Stalin: But there are many questions relating to the safety of our two countries which can be discussed between us.

Eden: We can discuss matters between us, but ultimately, for the purpose of the peace treaty, the Soviet Union, Great Britain, and the United States of America must all come in and agree with one another on the principal world affairs.

Stalin: I agree.

I then suggested that before we spoke of military plans, we ought to clear up a political point. Should we try to combine our two documents, or what course did Stalin propose.

Stalin: I think that what you have submitted is a kind of declaration, whereas ours are two agreements. A declaration I regard as algebra, but an agreement as practical arithmetic. I do not wish to decry algebra, but I prefer practical arithmetic, and I think in the present circumstances, when Hitler is boasting to everyone of all the treaties he has managed to obtain, it would be wiser to have treaties between the two countries, and our documents are in that form.

Eden: Perhaps I could take the two treaties as a basis and see if there is anything on our document which it is worth while incorporating in the two treaties.

Stalin: What about the attachment of the secret protocol [regarding postwar frontiers]?

Eden: My difficulty is that I cannot sign such a document without consulting my colleagues, and we have not as yet applied our minds to these problems.

Maisky: Not even the Soviet frontiers?

Eden: I couldn't do this without consulting the Prime Minister and also talking to the Americans. We could give an answer when I get back to London, which I could communicate to Mr. Maisky, and then we could continue with the discussion. . . .

Stalin then spoke of the possibility of dividing Germany, and giving Poland the lands up to the Oder.

Eden: There is a difficulty in cutting up Germany unless the movement for it comes from within the country, as you may cause an irredentist movement to unite the country again, rather like the *Anschluss*.

Stalin: These kind of conceptions brought us to the present war. Would you like to try another attack by Germany?

Eden: I think that is rather an over-simplification of the cause of the war. . . .

December 17th: . . . The conversation, which up to that moment had been smooth in character, suddenly changed and Stalin began to show his claws. He opened by asking for our immediate recognition of Russia's 1941 frontiers as the Soviet frontiers in the peace treaty. When I explained at length that I was not able to promise such a thing, Stalin retorted that, in that event, he would rather have no agreement. I replied that the Prime Minister [Churchill] had made a statement publicly to the whole world that we would not recognize changes made during the war. This was said when Germany was advancing and was really to the advantage of the U.S.S.R. Obviously I could not now decide this issue of frontiers although, as I had said, I was prepared to take it up when I returned to London.

Stalin: If you say that you might well say tomorrow that you do not recognize the Ukraine as forming part of the U.S.S.R.

Eden: That is a complete misunderstanding of the position. It is only changes from the pre-war frontiers that we do not recognize. The only change in the Ukraine is its occupation by Germany, so of course we accept the Ukraine as being part of the U.S.S.R. . . . Let me take the case of Canada and the question of the frontier between Poland and Russia. Canada sent us hundreds of thousands of soldiers to help in the war and if they were to hear tomorrow that I had agreed upon the Polish-Russian frontier, without any consultation with them, they would have every right to the strongest complaint. No Minister who did a thing like that could survive for twenty-four hours.

Stalin: I certainly do not want to demand the impossible from you and I fully realize the limitation of your powers, but I am addressing myself to the British Government and I am genuinely surprised. I thought that the Atlantic Charter was directed against those people who were trying to establish world dominion. It now looks as if the Charter was directed against the U.S.S.R. To this I [Eden] later replied:

Eden: If you were asking for the frontiers which existed in 1939, before the war broke out between us and Germany, there would be no difficulty at all, but now you are asking for frontiers which differ from those of 1939 in various places. I have taken note of that and will report it to my Government, but I cannot see how these agreements that it is proposed to sign will make it any more difficult for us to give you the answer that you want.

Stalin: It makes it look as if I should have to come cap in hand.

Eden: Not at all, I don't understand that. These are documents of perfect equality and don't represent the conferring of anything by either party upon the other.

Molotov: We are talking of common war aims, of what we are both fighting for. On one of these important aims, our western frontiers, we have no support from Great Britain.

7   FROM   *Cordell Hull*

The Moscow Conference Means the End of Balance of Power Politics (October–November 1943)

By the autumn of 1943 the Allies had taken the offensive in the war. On the Eastern front particularly, the Soviets scored a series of sustained victories over Nazi armies. In this context, the Allies prepared for two major diplomatic conferences. The first occurred in Moscow during the late October when the foreign ministers of the U.S., U.S.S.R., Great Britain, and China met. The central question was Poland's fate, but discussion was brief because the Soviets insisted on a "friendly" Polish government that would accept the Russian view of the Polish eastern boundary, that is, a boundary which would give a large portion of Poland, as it existed in August 1939, to the Soviet Union. Secretary of State Cordell Hull said little about Poland. He had

SOURCE. U.S. *Dept. of State Bulletin,* **IX** (November 20, 1943), pp. 341–345.

larger diplomatic objectives in view. Hull tried to obtain a Big Four agreement on a series of principles that would govern Allied diplomacy during the war. These principles perfectly implemented Luce's "American Century" and the Atlantic Charter. Hull reported on his success at the conference to the U.S. Congress on November 18, 1943. His speech is excerpted in the following document. To appreciate what Hull accomplished, or more precisely, what he failed to accomplish, the original American proposals must be analyzed. For example, Hull notes that the Big Four agreed "That after the termination of hostilities they will not employ their military forces within the territories of other states except for the purposes envisaged in this declaration and after joint consultation." Originally the words "and agreement" were added in the American draft, but Hull removed them after Molotov objected. The Soviets were not allowing any veto over their actions in Eastern Europe. Hull's euphoric speech to Congress must be read in the light of his failure to obtain agreement on Poland and, more generally, on Russian actions throughout Eastern Europe.

The second diplomatic conference occurred when Churchill, Roosevelt, and Stalin met at Teheran in November. On the Polish issue, Stalin proposed, and Churchill tentatively accepted, the moving of the Polish boundary deep into German territory so that the Poles could be recompensed for the territory they would lose to the Soviets. Roosevelt sat by quietly, later explaining to Stalin that he sympathized with the proposal but could do nothing because of six or seven million Polish votes which would be influential in the next Presidential election in the United States. On the question of Germany, Roosevelt and Stalin argued for drastic dismemberment into as many as five states, but Churchill refused to weaken Germany in this manner. No agreement was reached.

In view of the Soviet positions at Moscow and Teheran, what is the significance of Hull's phrase, "There will no longer be need for spheres of influence, for alliances, for balance of power"? Is the European Advisory Commission, as described by Hull, sufficiently powerful to end "spheres of influence"? Why does the Secretary of State move from the assumption that "each nation's own primary interest requires it to cooperate with the others?"

At the end of the war, each of the United Nations and each of the nations associated with them will have the same common interest in national security, in world order under law, in peace, in the full promotion of the political, economic, and social welfare of their respective peoples—in the principles and spirit of the Atlantic Charter and the Declaration by United Nations. The future of these indispensable common interests depends absolutely upon international cooperation. Hence, each nation's own primary interest requires it to cooperate with the others.

These considerations led the Moscow Conference to adopt the

four-nation declaration with which you are all familiar. I should like to comment briefly on its main provisions.

In that document, it was jointly declared by the United States, Great Britain, the Soviet Union, and China "That their united action, pledged for the prosecution of the war against their respective enemies, will be continued for the organization and maintenance of peace and security."

To this end, the four Governments declared that they "recognize the necessity of establishing at the earliest practicable date a general international organization, based on the principle of the sovereign equality of all peace-loving states, and open to membership by all such states, large and small." I should like to lay particular stress on this provision of the declaration. The principle of sovereign equality of all peace-loving states, irrespective of size and strength, as partners in a future system of general security will be the foundation stone upon which the future international organization will be constructed. . . .

The four Governments further agreed that, pending the inauguration in this manner of a permanent system of general security, "they will consult with one another and as occasion requires with other members of the United Nations with a view to joint action on behalf of the community of nations" whenever such action may be necessary for the purpose of maintaining international peace and security.

Finally, as an important self-denying ordinance, they declared "That after the termination of hostilities they will not employ their military forces within the territories of other states except for the purposes envisaged in this declaration and after joint consultation."

Through this declaration, the Soviet Union, Great Britain, the United States, and China have laid the foundation for cooperative effort in the post-war world toward enabling all peace-loving nations, large and small, to live in peace and security. . . .

As the provisions of the four-nation declaration are carried into effect, there will no longer be need for spheres of influence, for alliances, for balance of power, or any other of the special arrangements through which, in the unhappy past, the nations strove to safeguard their security or to promote their interests.

The Conference faced many political problems growing out of the military activities in Europe. It was foreseen that problems of common interest to our three Governments will continue to arise as our joint military efforts hasten the defeat of the enemy. . . . The Conference accordingly decided to set up a European Advisory Commission with its seat in London. This Commission will not of itself have executive powers. Its sole function will be to advise the Governments of the United States, Great Britain, and the Soviet Union. It is to deal with non-military problems relating to enemy territories and with such other problems as may be referred to it by the participating governments.

8 FROM   *State Department Officials on the Radio: The Importance of the Bretton Woods Agreements for Albert Lea, Minnesota (March 10, 1945)*

Secretary of State Cordell Hull mistakenly believed that he had obtained the political bases for postwar cooperation of the Big Four at the Moscow Conference. He was determined to find complementary economic bases. Hull did not believe that the world could be tranquil politically until it was calmed, then economically integrated and satisfied. His experiences as Secretary of State during the 1930s confirmed this conviction since he and most American officials thought World War II had been caused largely by the economic frictions arising out of the depression. The depression had especially led such nations as Germany, and to a lesser extent Great Britain and the United States, into a desperate search for economic amelioratives, and that search had resulted in forms of nationalism (as tariffs and exchange controls), which led to political conflict and an inability to cooperate in the international arena. No one wanted to endure the nightmare of 1929–1939 again. To Hull and other officials, a healthy American economy was imperative if the entire world system was to be restored properly after the war. The American and world economies were therefore interdependent, exactly as Henry Luce, among others, had noted in the early years of the war. How dependent American officials believed their nation was on the international economic system became clear at Bretton Woods, New Hampshire in the summer of 1944, when 44 nations gathered to hammer out principles and institutions for postwar economic cooperation. Soviet delegates attended as observers, but then and forever after refused to sign the agreements. Three top State Department officials explained the Bretton Woods Agreements in a special radio program during the early spring of 1945. What are the implied alternatives if the Bretton Woods principles do not work and the world economy, along with the United States system, begins a serious decline?

SOURCE. *Department of State Bulletin*, **XII** (March 11, 1945), pp. 401–407.

NATIONAL BROADCASTING COMPANY'S UNIVERSITY
OF THE AIR

Announcer: Our topic this time is "World Trade and World Peace," and the chairman of these State Department programs, Assistant Secretary of State Archibald MacLeish, is here with two other Assistant Secretaries—William L. Clayton, who is in charge of economic affairs, and Dean Acheson, who is responsible for congressional relations. And now . . .

MacLeish: This is Archibald MacLeish . . . Today the world can produce enough raw materials and enough finished goods to supply everybody in the world with all of necessities of life. Or rather it could, if we could find a way of getting the goods and the people together. . . . What would you say, Dean, is the main choice we have to make in our foreign economic policy?

Acheson: We have the same choice that we were faced with in last week's broadcast on Dumbarton Oaks [where the United Nations was founded]. The same alternatives are present. Are we going to aim at a collective security system with a world organized for peace; or are we going to fall back on the old system of "going it alone", with each nation relying on its own powers and resources to pull itself up at the expense of other nations. . . .

MacLeish: Well, let's go back to Bretton Woods. How will the Bretton Woods agreements help the disorganized and shattered world to function? You were there, Dean Acheson. Can you tell us about that?

Acheson: First, I'd like to fill in the background. I'll make it brief. In the twenties and thirties, nations discovered various monetary tricks which they employed to further their own national interests at the expense of other countries, all of which impeded the operation of the old international gold system. Eventually the gold system collapsed in all but a very few countries, and was replaced by a confused patchwork of currencies and exchange controls that played havoc with foreign trade.

MacLeish: I think you'd better explain that term *exchange controls*.

Acheson: They simply mean that no one is allowed to spend any money outside the country without permission of his government.

MacLeish: Can we expect anything different after this war is over?

Acheson: After the war, the United States can do one of two things: It can say that it will play the game of monetary devices and exchange controls itself. If we make that choice, we will be destroying the economies of other countries and the world will revert to a financial jungle. The Bretton Woods agreements are the other alternative. These agreements, which are the product of the experts of 44 countries, point the way out of chaos and economic warfare toward a new system based on cooperative action. To push these agreements aside is like dealing with a highly complicated irrigation problem by calling in a medicine man instead of using modern equipment such as dams and locks and irrigation canals.

MacLeish: Maybe you'd better describe the agreements before we go into the arguments about them.

Acheson: The Bretton Woods agreements provide for an International Bank and a Monetary Fund. This Fund, as proposed, is a substitute for international monetary warfare. Membership in the Monetary Fund requires the nations to agree to four primary propositions. The Fund says to each nation: First, will you agree to define your money in terms of gold? Second, will you agree to keep your money within one percent of its defined exchange value in terms of gold? Third, will you agree not to place restrictions on current transactions; that is, agree *not* to *prevent* your people from obtaining the currencies they need to pay for imports and meet other current obligations? And fourth, will you consult with the Fund whenever a problem comes up which you feel makes it necessary to change in any way the value of your currency? These points are basic elements of stability as envisaged at Bretton Woods.

Clayton: You might add, Mr. Acheson, that a change in the value of a particular country's currency is of importance not only to that country, but to all countries. When any one country starts tearing the fabric, the whole thing goes to pieces.

Acheson: That's right. Now, what this proposed Fund will do is this: It will create a big basket of currencies into which each country must put some of its own currency. Then, any nation which is a member of the Fund can come to that basket and obtain a limited amount of currency, that is, the currency of another nation, when it has need for it and cannot obtain it as a result of some temporary difficulty.

MacLeish: In other words, the Fund is an instrument to achieve security in the financial and economic fields—to give each country the strength of all through common use of the common reservoir.

Acheson: Yes, that's right. . . .

MacLeish: Now, what about the other half of the Bretton Woods agreements—the International Bank for Reconstruction and Development? As I understand it, the Bank's purpose would be to lend money to devastated and undeveloped countries. That would help to build them up until they can contribute more to world trade and the wealth of the family of nations. But how would the Bank be organized, Mr. Acheson?

Acheson: The capital stock of the International Bank would be subscribed to by all of the United Nations. The Bank will in some instances make direct loans, but most of its activities would consist in the guaranteeing of loans made by private investors through usual investment channels.

MacLeish: Couldn't all of this financing be handled by private investors?

Acheson: Most of it will be. But private investors might well feel that the risk involved was too great to warrant their making the loan. The International Bank can look at the problem of foreign lending from a broader basis. If the International Bank agrees that the loans are sound, it will guarantee these loans, even though they are made by private banking institutions. Then if there should be a default, the International Bank would make the loans good; but by virtue of the government guaranties, any loss would be spread among all the countries that are members of the Bank. It's like an insurance policy.

MacLeish: We are agreed that the Dumbarton Oaks Proposals and the Bretton Woods agreements are both based on the same concept of security through collective action. But isn't it also true, Mr. Acheson, that any real security must be based on an expanding economy. Isn't it true that unless there is a great expansion in the production of wealth, and a marked rise in the level of living, we can't be secure; and the entire world order is threatened?

Acheson: Yes, that's fundamental. . . .

MacLeish: Now, I'd like to ask Will Clayton: What does all this mean to John Anderson, who works in a meat-packing house out in Albert Lea, Minnesota? . . .

Clayton: Today we are exporting over 14 billion dollars' worth of goods a year. We simply *can't afford* after this war to let our trade drop off to the 2- or 3-billion figure it hit in 1932 during the depression. That would make another depression almost certain, and John Anderson certainly wouldn't like that. But that's just what will happen if we come to the end of the war without a well-rounded foreign economic program.

MacLeish: And how would you define that well-rounded program?

Clayton: To build up foreign commerce, and to remove barriers that stand in the way, whether they are government barriers or private barriers.

MacLeish: It's pretty plain that you both think of foreign economic policy and domestic economic policy as being so closely related that they amount to the same thing. But how are you going to persuade John Anderson that his job depends on foreign trade?

Clayton: I think there are two principal reasons why John Anderson, and everyone else in the United States, should be interested in foreign trade. In the first place, a lot of the products John Anderson packs find their way overseas. As far as the rest of the country is concerned, there are whole regions whose products normally move extensively in foreign trade and whose prosperity depends on this trade. The South, for instance. The South is deeply interested in foreign trade because the people there raise more cotton and tobacco than this country has ever been able to use. . . .

Acheson: And the same is true of the West Coast. We used to ship abroad almost half of the prunes raised in California. We exported two thirds of the wheat raised in the Pacific Northwest; and apples from out there were also one of our top exports. Take away the foreign trade on these items and prices collapse and the whole region's economy is disrupted. I think you had a second reason, Will?

Clayton: I was going to add that John Anderson's job will probably depend on a high level of production after the war; and we can't have that unless we have markets for our goods. It's true that the greatest market for American goods is in the United States, but in some things our productive capacity is so great that the United States alone can't absorb all of it.

MacLeish: Mr. Clayton, what would be the value of the goods you figure we must sell abroad each year after the war in order to achieve a high level of employment?

Clayton: Some of our best economists estimate that we would probably have to sell 10 billion dollars' worth of goods a year abroad if we want to have relatively high level employment and a national income in the neighborhood of 150 billion dollars. In other words, we've got to export three times as much as we exported just before the war, if we want to keep our industry running at somewhere near capacity. . . .

Acheson: I think you can say that in industry every tenth job depends on foreign trade. If you work in a machine shop with 2,000 workers, for example, the chances are that 200 of the people in your plant will have their jobs lopped off if our foreign trade drops off to almost nothing.

MacLeish: That puts it clearly, especially for industries with large exports, Mr. Acheson. But how about John Anderson, out in Albert Lea, Minnesota. . . . ? Why should he worry about losing his job?

Acheson: Because, even if none of the products that Anderson packs were shipped out of the country, he would have to sell them somewhere. Now, if that machine shop we were talking about has a full staff of 2,000 people at work, perhaps they'll buy 2,000 hams a month. But if 200 of them were to be laid off, John Anderson's packing plant and others like it will probably sell only 1,800 hams to that same group of people the next month. . . .

MacLeish: I'd like to ask Will Clayton about reciprocal trade agreements. Haven't they been fairly successful in lowering tariff walls?

Clayton: They have accomplished a great deal [since they were begun by the New Deal in 1934]. The average rate of duty on goods affected by the tariff has been reduced almost one third—from about 48 percent to about 33 percent. The records show that up to the beginning of the war our trade improved substantially due to trade agreements.

MacLeish: Do you mind explaining how the reciprocal trade agreements law works?

Clayton: It's very simple, actually. The law has been in effect for over 10 years now. It authorizes the President to sign agreements with other countries, whereby we cut tariffs that interfere unduly with their export to us, and they do the same for us. . . .

MacLeish: To sum up our discussion, our foreign economic policy is intimately tied up with the Dumbarton Oaks Proposals for an international security organization. The idea behind Dumbarton Oaks is that the peace-loving nations of the world must get together to underwrite a permanent peace. But we won't be able to do this unless we build economic peace at the same time. The two go hand in hand. An expanding world trade is one of the foundations of world peace.

Clayton: You might say the Dumbarton Oaks plan will provide police protection for the world community and much in the Bretton Woods Proposals suggests a world-wide building and loan association.

9   FROM   *Milovan Djilas*
Stalin in 1944–1945

As Washington officials led the drive for the Bretton Woods agreements and Anglo-American armies began the liberation of Western Europe, Russian troops were moving rapidly over Eastern Europe, and Josef Stalin was planning his own postwar world. He kept Soviet financial resources and plans out of the hands and beyond the eyes of international agencies. His primary concerns were revealed rather melodramatically and privately to Milovan Djilas, a top Yugoslav Communist official in 1944–1945 who came to know Stalin well during several trips to Moscow. In the following selection, what is the Soviet leader's primary diplomatic priority? Note carefully Djilas' analysis of Stalin's revolutionary views. What do these views imply about Soviet policies in areas outside the reach of the Red Army?

Stalin presented his views on the distinctive nature of the war that was being waged: "This war is not as in the past; whoever occupies a territory also imposes on it his own social system. Everyone imposes his own system as far as his army can reach. It cannot be otherwise."

He also pointed out, without going into long explanations, the meaning of his Panslavic policy. "If the Slavs keep united and maintain solidarity, no one in the future will be able to move a finger. Not even a finger!" he repeated, emphasizing his thought by cleaving the air with his forefinger.

Someone expressed doubt that the Germans would be able to recuperate within fifty years. But Stalin was of a different opinion. "No, they will recover, and very quickly. That is a highly developed industrial country with an extremely qualified and numerous working class and technical intelligentsia. Give them twelve to fifteen years and they'll be on their feet again. And this is why the unity of the Slavs is important. But even apart from this, if the unity of the Slavs exists, no one will dare move a finger."

At one point he got up, hitched up his pants as though he was about to wrestle or to box, and cried out almost in a transport, "The war shall soon be over. We shall recover in fifteen or twenty years, and then we'll have another go at it."

SOURCE. Milovan Djilas, *Conversations with Stalin*, Translated from the Serbo-Croat by Michael B. Petrovich (New York: 1962), pp. 114–115, 132–133. Reprinted by permission of Harcourt, Brace and World, Inc., Publishers.

There was something terrible in his words: a horrible war was still going on. Yet there was something impressive, too, about his cognizance of the paths he had to take, the inevitability that faced the world in which he lived and the movement that he headed. . . .

It is time something was said about Stalin's attitude toward revolutions. . . . Because Moscow abstained, always in decisive moments, from supporting the Chinese, Spanish, and in many ways even the Yugoslav revolutions, the view prevailed, not without reason, that Stalin was generally against revolutions. This is, however, not entirely correct. He was opposed only conditionally, that is, to the degree to which the revolution went beyond interests of the Soviet state. He felt instinctively that the creation of revolutionary centers outside of Moscow could endanger its supremacy in world Communism, and of course that is what actually happened. That is why he helped revolutions only up to a certain point—up to where he could control them—but he was always ready to leave them in the lurch whenever they slipped out of his grasp. I maintain that not even today is there any essential change in this respect in the policy of the Soviet Government.

A man who had subjected all activities in his own country to his views and to his personality, Stalin could not behave differently outside. Having identified domestic progress and freedom with the interests and privileges of a political party, he could not act in foreign affairs other than as a hegemonist. As with everyone, handsome is as handsome does. He became himself the slave of the despotism, the bureaucracy, the narrowness, and the servility that he imposed on his country.

It is indeed true that no one can take freedom from another without losing his own.

10   FROM   *Churchill and Stalin*
Dividing the Balkans on a Half-Sheet of Paper
(October 9, 1944)

As Soviet armies swept across Eastern Europe, Winston Churchill became concerned over the power that these conquests would give Stalin. The Prime Minister was especially determined to keep Greece and the Eastern Mediterranean, the so-called lifeline of the British Empire, out of the Soviet sphere of influence. In early October 1944, Churchill flew to Moscow and on the ninth began a series of conferences with Stalin regarding which power should be primarily responsible for reconstructing specific areas of Eastern Europe. In the following selection, Churchill vividly recalls the progress of the first session with Stalin. The United States did not officially participate in the meetings, although the American Ambassador to the Soviet Union, W. Averell Harriman, attended as an observer. Washington was appalled at the results of the talks. Roosevelt finally cabled that Churchill and Stalin must understand that he (the President) could not be bound by the agreement. Although Soviet and British subordinates continued to haggle over the exact figures, the Churchill-Stalin percentages became the general guide for appropriate Allied committees. What is the practical meaning of Churchill's statement, "Of course we had long and anxiously considered our point, and were only dealing with immediate war-time arrangements"?

We alighted at Moscow on the afternoon of October 9, and were received very heartily and with full ceremonial by Molotov and many high Russian personages. This time we were lodged in Moscow itself, with every care and comfort. I had one small, perfectly appointed house, and Anthony another near by. We were glad to dine alone together and rest. At ten o'clock that night we held our first important meeting in the Kremlin. . . .

The moment was apt for business, so I said, "Let us settle about our affairs in the Balkans. Your armies are in Rumania and Bulgaria. We have interests, missions, and agents there. Don't let us get at cross-purposes in small ways. So far as Britain and Russia are concerned, how would it do for you to have ninety per cent predominance in Rumania, for us to have ninety per cent of the say in Greece, and go fifty-fifty about Yugoslavia?" While this was being translated I wrote out on a half-sheet of paper:

SOURCE. Winston S. Churchill, *Triumph and Tragedy* (Cambridge, Mass.: 1953), pp. 226–228. Reprinted by permission of Houghton Mifflin Company, Boston.

Rumania	
Russia	90%
The others	10%
Greece	
Great Britain	90%
(in accord with U.S.A.)	
Russia	10%
Yugoslavia	50–50%
Hungary	50–50%
Bulgaria	
Russia	75%
The others	25%

I pushed this across to Stalin, who had by then heard the translation. There was a slight pause. Then he took his blue pencil and made a large tick upon it, and passed it back to us. It was all settled in no more time than it takes to set down.

Of course we had long and anxiously considered our point, and were only dealing with immediate war-time arrangements. All larger questions were reserved on both sides for what we then hoped would be a peace table when the war was won.

After this there was a long silence. The pencilled paper lay in the centre of the table. At length I said, "Might it not be thought rather cynical if it seemed we had disposed of these issues, so fateful to millions of people, in such an offhand manner? Let us burn the paper." "No, you keep it," said Stalin.

11 FROM *The Big Three at Yalta*
The Declaration on Liberated Europe

The Soviets followed up the Stalin-Churchill percentage deal by virtually excluding Anglo-American officials from the important control commissions in liberated Hungary, Rumania, and Bulgaria. The Soviets also had another precedent for their actions; in Italy, the conquering Anglo-American forces had excluded Russians from any important role in reconstruction. American officials at the Yalta Conference (February 1945) attempted to reopen the question of Anglo-American rights in liberated Eastern Europe

SOURCE. U.S. Dept. of State, *Foreign Relations of the United States, The Conferences at Malta and Yalta, 1945* (Washington: 1955), pp. 977–978.

by having the Soviets agree to the Declaration on Liberated Europe. This Declaration specifically resurrected the Atlantic Charter principles. When the American draft was given to Churchill and Stalin, the British leader said he would accept it as long as everyone understood that the Atlantic Charter did not apply to the British Empire. Stalin and his Foreign Minister, V. M. Molotov, insisted on a fundamental change. They requested that a clause which indicated that the Big Three had equal rights in any dispute be changed to a provision for mutual consultations. That meant that the de facto power in any liberated country, such as Rumania, lay in the occupying armies which merely had to consult with other agencies. American officials were most reluctant to accept that interpretation. Does the Declaration, as the State Department later insisted, oblige the Big Three to "concert their policies in assisting the liberated peoples"?

The Premier of the Union of Soviet Socialist Republics, the Prime Minister of the United Kingdom and the President of the United States of America have consulted with each other in the common interests of the peoples of their countries and those of liberated Europe. They jointly declare their mutual agreement to concert during the temporary period of instability in liberated Europe the policies of their three governments in assisting the peoples liberated from the domination of Nazi Germany and the peoples of the former Axis satellite states of Europe to solve by democratic means their pressing political and economic problems.

The establishment of order in Europe and the re-building of national economic life must be achieved by processes which will enable the liberated peoples to destroy the last vestiges of Nazism and Fascism and to create democratic institutions of their own choice. This is a principle of the Atlantic Charter—the right of all peoples to choose the form of government under which they will live—the restoration of sovereign rights and self-government to those peoples who have been forcibly deprived of them by the aggressor nations.

To foster the conditions in which the liberated peoples may exercise these rights, the three governments will jointly assist the people in any European liberated state or former Axis satellite state in Europe where in their judgment conditions require (a) to establish conditions of internal peace; (b) to carry out emergency measures for the relief of distressed peoples; (c) to form interim governmental authorities broadly representative of all democratic elements in the population and pledged to the earliest possible establishment through free elections of governments responsive to the will of the people; and (d) to facilitate where necessary the holding of such elections.

The three governments will consult the other United Nations and provisional authorities or other governments in Europe when matters of direct interest to them are under consideration.

When, in the opinion of the three governments, conditions in any European liberated state or any former Axis satellite state in Europe make such action necessary, they will immediately consult together on the measures necessary to discharge the joint responsibilities set forth in this declaration.

By this declaration we reaffirm our faith in the principles of the Atlantic Charter, our pledge in the Declaration by the United Nations, and our determination to build in co-operation with other peace-loving nations world order under law, dedicated to peace, security, freedom and general well-being of all mankind.

In issuing this declaration, the Three Powers express the hope that the Provisional Government of the French Republic may be associated with them in the procedure suggested.

12   FROM   *U.S. Department of State*
The Soviets Tie Up Economic Activities
in the Balkans (May 30, 1945)

In mid-April, 1945, a widely publicized Soviet article argued that the Russians were abiding by the Declaration of Liberated Europe because they were eliminating the pro-Fascist political parties and thereby preparing Eastern Europe for democratic government. Although the Soviets continued to exclude Anglo-American officials from the more powerful control commissions in the Russian sphere, political activity throughout the liberated areas produced varying results. After vacillating in handling Rumania (which historically has lost little love on the Russians), Stalin forced that country to establish a government acceptable to Communist interests. In Hungary, however, an election in November resulted in a majority vote for the anti-Russian Small Holders' party and only 17 percent for the Communists. Stalin did nothing to repeal the results of that balloting. His economic policy was more uniform and less tolerant. Given their view of the dynamics in the international situation, American officials interpreted that economic policy as contrary to the Atlantic Charter and, therefore, to long-term United

SOURCE. U.S. Dept. of State, *Foreign Relations of the United States, 1945, Volume V, Europe* (Washington, D.C.: 1967), pp. 852–853.

States interests. The following selection, written by Elbridge Durbrow, Chief of the State Department's Division of Eastern European Affairs, illustrates the American concern. Did Soviet agreement to the Declaration on Liberated Europe give Durbrow grounds for complaint about Soviet economic activity in Eastern Europe?

MEMORANDUM BY THE CHIEF OF THE DIVISION OF EASTERN EUROPEAN AFFAIRS, MAY 30, 1945

In view of the United States government's announced policy of liberalizing trade in the post-war world and the efforts now being made to obtain from Congress authorization to reduce tariffs by an additional fifty percent in connection with the trade agreement policy, it is believed that careful thought and consideration must immediately be given to the restrictive trade policies the Soviet Government is putting into effect in eastern and southeastern Europe.

We have just received, through unofficial channels, what we believe to be the full texts of the recently-concluded Soviet-Bulgarian and Soviet-Rumanian Trade Agreements. As far as I am aware, we have not as yet received a copy of the recently-concluded Soviet-Finnish Trade Agreement. The general tenor of these agreements is very restrictive and are apparently aimed at excluding free trade in these areas by other powers. The agreements are in effect barter agreements and the prices for the goods delivered by the smaller countries are apparently very low. Moreover, provision is made in the Rumanian agreement, for instance, for the creation of jointly-owned Rumanian-Soviet concerns to exploit the oil, mineral and other resources of the country and provision is made for the creation of a joint Rumanian-Soviet bank which apparently might be used to control the entire financial structure of Rumania.

I believe it is fair to assume that the Soviet Government will make similar agreements with all other countries in the areas under its control and that by this method they will create an almost airtight economic blackout in the entire area east of the Stettin-Trieste line. This blackout, coupled with the effective news blackout in this area, presents a very serious problem which we must give immediate consideration to. [Signed] Elbridge Durbrow.

13   FROM   *Foreign Minister V. M. Molotov*

A Russian View of "Equal Opportunity"
(October 10, 1946)

To most Americans, Elbridge Durbrow's plea for "liberalizing trade in the post-war world" seemed fair and unexceptionable. He was merely restating the phrases of Henry Luce and the Atlantic Charter. In the selection that follows, however, V. M. Molotov, Foreign Minister of the Soviet Union, raised vigorous objection to the United States' economic policies. In doing so he also attacked the American conception of the world that was embodied in the Atlantic Charter, the Bretton Woods pacts, and the Declaration on Liberated Europe. Molotov delivered this selection as part of a speech at the Paris Peace Conference in the autumn of 1946. The conference was discussing a peace treaty for Rumania, and the United States had been pushing for a recognition of "equal opportunity" in economic affairs of Eastern Europe. What political results does Molotov see if the "equal opportunity" doctrine is inserted in the peace treaty?

SPEECH AT PARIS PEACE CONFERENCE, OCTOBER 10, 1946

The principle of so-called "equal opportunity" has become a favourite topic of late. What, it is argued, could be better than this principle, which would establish equal opportunity for all states without discrimination? The advocates of this view come forward now as modern champions of the principle of equality in relations between states. But in that case, gentlemen, let us discuss the principle of equality seriously and honestly. . . .

Here in Paris everyone of you can find a copy of the "World Almanac, 1946." In this book you may read the following figures: the national income of the U.S.A. in 1941 was estimated at 96,000 million dollars, in 1942 at 122,000 million dollars, in 1943 at 149,000 million dollars, and in 1944 at 160,000 million dollars. Thus, in four years of the war the national income of the U.S.A. rose by 64,000 million dollars. The same book says that in 1938 the total national income of the United States was 64,000 million dollars. Hence the mere increase in the national income of the U.S.A. during the war

SOURCE. V. M. Molotov, *Problems of Foreign Policy, Speeches and Statements, April 1945–November 1948* (MOSCOW: 1949), pp. 210–216.

years was equal to its total national income in 1938. These are facts which one cannot refrain from mentioning. . . .

We know that the United States made a very great effort in this war, in defence of its own interests and of our common aims, for which we are all very grateful to the United States. But for all that, it cannot be said that the United States is one of those states which suffered grave material damage in the second world war, which were ruined and weakened in this war. We are glad that this did not happen to our ally, although we ourselves have had to go through trying times, the consequences of which will take us long years to heal.

Now that you know the facts, place side by side Rumania, enfeebled by the war, or Yugoslavia, ruined by the German and Italian fascists, and the United States of America, whose wealth has grown immensely during the war, and you will clearly see what the implementation of the principle of "equal opportunity" would mean in practice. Imagine, under these circumstances, that in this same Rumania or Yugoslavia, or in some other war-weakened state, you have this so-called "equal opportunity" for, let us say, American capital—that is, the opportunity for it to penetrate unhindered into Rumanian industry, or Yugoslav industry and so forth: what, then, will remain of Rumania's national industry, or of Yugoslavia's national industry?

It is surely not so difficult to understand that if American capital were given a free hand in the small states ruined and enfeebled by the war, as the advocates of the principle of "equal opportunity" desire, American capital would buy up the local industries, appropriate the more attractive Rumanian, Yugoslav and all other enterprises, and would become the master in these small states. Given such a situation, we would probably live to see the day when in your own country, on switching on the radio, you would be hearing not so much your own language as one American gramophone record after another or some piece or other of British propaganda. The time might come when in your own country, on going to the cinema, you would be seeing American films sold for foreign consumption—and not those of the better quality, but those manufactured in greater quantity, and circulated and imposed abroad by the agents of powerful firms and cinema companies which have grown particularly rich during the war.

Can anyone really fail to see that if, as a result of the application of the principle of so-called "equal opportunity" in small states, unrestricted competition begins between the home products and the products poured out by the factories of the United States or Great Britain, nothing will remain of the sovereignty and independence of these states, especially considering the postwar conditions? Is it not clear that such unrestricted application of the principle of "equal opportunity" in the given conditions would in practice mean the veritable economic enslavement of the small states and their subjugation to the rule and arbitrary will of strong and enriched foreign firms, banks and industrial companies? Is it not clear that if such "principles of equality" are applied in international economic life, the smaller states will be governed by the orders, injunctions, instructions of strong foreign trusts and monopolies? Was this what we fought for when we battled the fascist invaders, the Hitlerite and Japanese imperialists?

14   FROM   *U.S. Department of State:*
              The Threat of International Communism
              to Europe and the United States
                    (June 2, 1945)

Besides differences over political and economic issues, there existed, of course, a deep ideological division between the United States and the Soviet Union. In August, 1920, Woodrow Wilson's Secretary of State, Bainbridge Colby, announced that the United States could not recognize the new Soviet Government because "the existing regime in Russia is based upon the negation of every principle of honor and good faith, and every usage and convention, underlying the whole structure of international law. . . . Indeed, upon numerous occasions, the responsible spokesman of this Power, and its official agencies, have declared that . . . the maintenance of their own rule, depends, and must continue to depend, upon the occurrence of revolutions in all other great civilized nations, including the United States, which will overthrow and destroy their governments and set up Bolshevist rule in their stead." Thirteen years later Franklin D. Roosevelt's administration finally recognized the Soviets, but this fear of Communist doctrine hardly diminished. After Hitler invaded Russia in June, 1941, the State Department announced that it would aid the Soviets, but added that "principles and doctrines of communistic dictatorship are as intolerable and as alien to their own beliefs [*that is, the beliefs of Americans*], *as are the principles and doctrines of Nazi dictatorship." These ideological divisions were hushed after Pearl Harbor. The Soviets disbanded the Communist International (or Comintern) on May 22, 1943; since 1919 this organization had directed Communist parties throughout the world under*

SOURCE. U.S. Dept. of State, *Foreign Relations of the United States, the Conference of Berlin,* **I** (Washington, D.C.: 1960), pp. 278–280.

Moscow's leadership, although the Russians had usually denied Moscow's role. Western observers, particularly in the State Department, doubted that the effect of the 1943 announcement would be an actual decrease in international Communist activity. Stalin had just shaken the West by suddenly cutting relations with the Polish government-in-exile in London, and Washington officials tended to see the dissolution of the Comintern as simply his attempt to reassure the West of his goodwill. The American fear became especially apparent in dealing with left-wing political groups in the liberated areas of Western Europe. The United States did not wish to see the Nazis replaced in France or Italy, for example, with left-wing politicians who would be sympathetic to Communists. As the following selection reveals, the State Department fully understood that the chaos left in the wake of the war would be conducive to leftist and Communist elements in Europe. The selection was part of a long memorandum on the American and other Communist parties, prepared in the State Department and sent to President Truman for his consideration as he prepared for the Potsdam Conference. Scholars, particularly Gar Alperovitz and Gabriel Kolko, have cast considerable doubt on the memorandum's claim that the American Communists had been instructed from abroad to begin attacking United States postwar plans. What are the unsaid assumptions underlying the last two sentences of this selection?

CONDITIONS IN EUROPE FAVORABLE FOR THE DEVELOPMENT OF THE COMMUNIST MOVEMENT

The smoothly-functioning, experienced and disciplined communist machine has been demonstrated. At the end of the last World War the Communists had no such machine. Hence, from an operational viewpoint, the apparatus is in position to take advantage immediately of any opportunities which may be presented. In fact the elite of the communist refugees have returned to their respective countries after several years of safe haven and training in Moscow. These elements are far more skillful than any this country can propose.

To a Communist, Europe today politically and economically represents a perfect situation for the propagation of their doctrines. Dean Inge [William Ralph, Dean of St. Paul's, London] has cogently expressed the feature which makes for communist success. He said, "In their quest for security, people will accept serfdom."

Europe is emerging from probably the most devastating war in its history. Concomitantly, the Red Army's exploits have been so well advertised that the majority of Europeans regard them as their liberators. Even in the West the Red Army receives the major share of the credit, thanks to the publicity given it by the communist press. The excesses of the Nazi regime and the fear of a rejuvenated Germany impel most Europeans to gravitate naturally toward the strongest remaining power in Europe—the Soviet Union. Furthermore, almost all Europeans have been living under totalitarian regimes, causing their thinking to be so conditioned at this time that the transition to another totalitarian regime is perfectly natural. The same situation may be true of Germany itself.

In addition, press censorship and radio control (always effective instruments of totalitarians) will again be utilized for that purpose.

Hitler's actions in thoroughly mixing up the economy of Europe, merging its various industries under Goering and seizing and consolidating banks serve now to facilitate the growth of communism, for it is an herculean if not impossible task to unscramble the mixup and find the original owners. Likewise, there is so much poverty and destitution in Europe that the mere possession of a better than average standard of living is viewed with suspicion by the masses. Europe affords now a perfect background for spontaneous class hatred to be channeled by a skillful agitator.

The thesis of the communist agitator in these circumstances has been praise of the Soviet Union as the liberator of the oppressed masses and the logical guarantor against a repetition of the causes. Consequently, each European country, it is emphasized, should align itself with the Soviet Union.

Simultaneously, the inhabitants of the afflicted countries expect the United States to feed them at least for the next year and provide machinery and credits for the rehabilitation of their economy. Communist parties, including that in the United States, emphasize in their propaganda that this role of the United States as almoner for Europe is a duty. Altruism is not expected to pay dividends even of good will.

POSSIBLE EFFECT ON THE UNITED STATES OF
CHANGE IN POLICY

While conjectural, it is possible to anticipate certain changes towards this country. Some changes are already clear. An attempt will be made to enumerate and describe possible changes.

1. Attacks on the Administration on grounds of abandoning the policies of the late President. Communists reserve for themselves the interpretation of the late President's policies.

2. Attacks on top personnel of State Department on grounds they are anti-Russian.

3. Use of communist underground in government departments to obtain confidential information.

4. Use of communist-controlled unions in key industries to strike if necessary, apparently for economic demands, actually for political purposes.

5. Use of communist apparatus in certain European countries to interfere with administration of our sphere of occupied Germany and perhaps to interfere with supply line of our troops.

The foregoing can be amplified considerably but it is unnecessary as the damage that can be done under the points enumerated would be serious. Now that an American organization has announced that it may have to change its tactics because one phase of the war is over, this Government is challenged. To recognize such a group as un-American, a potential fifth column with foreign allegiance, and to deal with it accordingly would be realistic. Decisive action against the American Communists would be a convincing demonstration to Stalin of the inherent strength of this country and would strengthen relations between the two countries.

15 FROM *Hopkins-Stalin Talks: Issues Dividing the United States and the Soviet Union (May 26 to June 6, 1945)*

By the late spring of 1945, the failure of the United States and the Soviet Union to agree on the application of the Declaration on Liberated Europe and the need for trade liberalization in the Russian zones of Eastern Europe, as well as American fear of international Communism, had poisoned East-West relations. Harry S. Truman, who became President after Franklin D. Roosevelt's death on April 12, 1945, agreed with Churchill that a Big Three summit meeting was needed to deal with the worsening problems. As part of the preparations for such a meeting (which would be held at Potsdam in July), Truman sent Harry Hopkins to thrash out some of the issues with Stalin. Hopkins had been Roosevelt's closest foreign policy advisor during the war, and the Russians viewed him as a person who understood their own difficulties. Hopkins

SOURCE. U.S. Department of State, *Foreign Relations of the United States, The Conference of Berlin*, **I** (Washington, D.C.: 1960), pp. 26–59.

was a physically sick man, but left a hospital bed to take this last mission. Poland and Germany emerged as the major issues, but the two men also discussed a series of lesser problems (whether Argentina should be admitted to the United Nations, whether smaller nations in the U.N.—such as Honduras and Puerto Rico—should have votes equal on critical questions to the votes of the three major powers, the apparent attempt by the United States to exert pressure on the Russians by suddenly stopping lend-lease). The tone of the discussion is also significant. What is the importance of Hopkins' statement, "the interests of the United States were world wide and not confined to North and South America and the Pacific Ocean"?

Mr. Hopkins then said that a few days ago President Truman had sent for him and had asked him to come to Moscow to have a talk with Marshal Stalin. . . . Two months ago there had been overwhelming sympathy among the American people for the Soviet Union and complete support for President Roosevelt's policies which the Marshal knew so well. . . . He said he wished to assure the Marshal with all the earnestness at his command that this body of American public opinion who had been the constant support of the Roosevelt policies were seriously disturbed about their relations with Russia. In fact, in the last six weeks deterioration of public opinion had been so serious as to affect adversely the relations between our two countries. [. . He said that, as the Marshal was aware, the cardinal basis of President Roosevelt's policy which the American people had fully supported had been the concept that the interests of the United States were world wide and not confined to North and South America and the Pacific Ocean and it was this concept that had led to the many conferences concerning the peace of the world which President Roosevelt had had with Marshal Stalin. President Roosevelt had believed that the Soviet Union had likewise world-wide interests and that the two countries could work out together any political or economic considerations at issue between them. *. . He said in a country like ours public opinion is affected by specific incidents and in this case the deterioration in public opinion in regard to our relations with the Soviet Union had been centered in our inability to carry into effect the Yalta Agreement on Poland. There were also a train of events, each unimportant in themselves, which had grown up around the Polish question, which contributed to the deterioration in public opinion. . . .

Marshal Stalin replied that the reason for the failure on the Polish question was that the Soviet Union desired to have a friendly Poland, but that Great Britain wanted to revive the system of *cordon sanitaire* on the Soviet borders. . . .

Mr. Hopkins stated that the United States would desire a Poland friendly to the Soviet Union and in fact desired to see friendly countries all along the Soviet borders.

Marshal Stalin replied if that be so we can easily come to terms in regard to Poland. . . .

Marshal Stalin said he would not attempt to use Soviet public opinion as a screen but would speak of the feeling that had been created in Soviet governmental circles as a result of recent moves on the part of the United States Government. He said these circles felt a certain alarm in regard to the attitude of the United States Government. It was their impression that the American attitude towards the Soviet Union had perceptibly cooled once it became obvious that Germany was defeated, and that it was as though the Americans were saying that the Russians were no longer needed. He said he would give the following examples:

1. The case of Argentina and the invitation to the San Francisco Conference. At Yalta it had been agreed that only those states which had declared war on Germany before the first of March would be invited but at San Francisco this decision had been overturned [when Argentina was invited]. He said it was not understood in the Soviet Union why Argentina could not have been asked to wait three months or so before joining the world organization. He added that the action of the Conference and the attitude of the United States had raised the question of the value of agreements between the three major powers if their decisions could be overturned by the votes of such countries as Honduras and Puerto Rico.

2. The question of the Reparations Commission. At Yalta it had been agreed that the three powers would sit on this Commission in Moscow and subsequently the United States Government had insisted that France should be represented on the same basis as the Soviet Union. This he felt was an insult to the Soviet Union in view of the fact that France had concluded a separate peace with Germany [in 1940] and had opened the frontier to the Germans. . . .

3. The attitude of the United States Government towards the Polish question. He said that at Yalta it had been agreed that the existing government was to be reconstructed and that anyone with common sense could see that this meant that the present government [dominated by the Polish Communists] was to form the basis of the

new. He said no other understanding of the Yalta Agreement was possible. Despite the fact that they were simple people the Russians should not be regarded as fools, which was a mistake the West frequently made, nor were they blind and could quite well see what was going on before their eyes. . . .

4. The manner in which Lend Lease had been curtailed. He said that if the United States was unable to supply the Soviet Union further under Lend Lease that was one thing but that the manner in which it had been done had been unfortunate and even brutal. For example, certain ships had been unloaded and while it was true that this order had been cancelled the whole manner in which it had been done had caused concern to the Soviet Government. If the refusal to continue Lend Lease was designed as pressure on the Russians in order to soften them up then it was a fundamental mistake. . . .

5. The disposition of the German Navy and merchant fleet which surrendered to the Allies. . . . As regards to the German fleet which had caused so much damage to Leningrad and other Soviet ports not one had been turned over to the Russians despite the fact the fleet had surrendered. He added that he had sent a message to the President and Prime Minister suggesting that at least one-third of the German Navy and merchant marine thus surrendered be turned over to the Soviet Union. . . .

Mr. Hopkins said he first of all wished to express his appreciation of the frankness with which Marshal Stalin had exposed his worries. . . . He said he would take the case of the German fleet first. . . . He also said that he had always understood that the fleet was to be divided between the United States, the Soviet Union and Great Britain. . . . [As regards the problem of Lend Lease] there had naturally been considerable confusion in the United States Government as to the status of Lend Lease towards Russia at the end of the war and that there had been varying legal interpretations but that he wished to emphasize that the incident to which Marshal Stalin referred did not have any fundamental policy significance. . . . He wished to assure the Marshal that however unfortunate an impression this question had caused in the mind of the Soviet Government he must believe that there was no attempt or desire on the part of the United States to use it as a pressure weapon. He said the United States is a strong power and does not go in for those methods. Furthermore, we have no conflict of immediate interests with the Soviet Union and would have no reason to adopt such practices. . . . [On the problem of France having a seat on the

Reparations Commission] so far as he knew our only motive was that France was to be represented on the Control Council for Germany and therefore appeared reasonable and logical that she should participate in the reparations discussions. He said he realized that the Soviet Union had reluctantly agreed to the participation of France in the Control Council at the Crimea Conference. In any event the situation now was that the three powers were to go ahead and begin discussions in Moscow without France. . . . [After some discussion of the Argentine question] Marshal Stalin said in any event what had been done could not be put right and that the Argentine question belonged to the past. . . .

16 FROM *Secretary of War*
Henry Stimson to President Truman
"The Only Way You Can Make a Man Trustworthy
is to Trust Him" (September 11, 1945)

As detailed in Chapters IV and V below, the Potsdam Conference failed to ameliorate Russian-American relations, particularly on the central issues of Poland and Germany. Nor were affairs improved in August. The American dropping of two atomic bombs on Japan, and the failure of Washington officials to share control of the bomb with the Allies, did nothing to lessen developing Soviet hostility. Meanwhile, the tightening Russian grip on Eastern Europe and the rapid Soviet victories in the Far East, gained after Russia declared war on Japan in early August, aroused new fears in the United States. Among Truman's advisors, Secretary of War Henry Stimson had taken the lead throughout the spring and summer of 1945 to formulate a tough policy line toward the Soviet Union. The failure of Potsdam and the events in August caused Stimson to reassess his ideas, particularly his view that the Russians could have no share in controlling the atomic bomb until they made major changes in their internal politics and international policies. On the eve of his retirement after fifty years of distinguished governmental service, Stimson, in the following selection, urged the President to follow different policies in dealing with Russia. If followed, what would be the effect of Stimson's policy in Russian-controlled areas of Eastern Europe?

SOURCE. U.S. Dept. of State, *Foreign Relations of the United States, 1945, Volume II, General: Political and Economic Matters* (Washington, D.C.: 1967), pp. 41–44.

THE SECRETARY OF WAR (STIMSON) TO PRESIDENT TRUMAN,
SEPTEMBER 11, 1945

Dear Mr. President: In handing you today my memorandum about our relations with Russia in respect to the atomic bomb, I am not unmindful of the fact that when in Potsdam I talked with you about the question whether we could be safe in sharing the atomic bomb with Russia while she was still a police state and before she put into effect provisions assuring personal rights of liberty to the individual citizen.

I still recognize the difficulty and am still convinced of the importance of the ultimate importance of a change in Russian attitude toward individual liberty but I have come to the conclusion that it would not be possible to use our possession of the atomic bomb as a direct lever to produce the change. I have become convinced that any demand by us for an internal change in Russia as a condition of sharing in the atomic weapon would be so resented that it would make the objective we have in view less probable.

I believe that the change in attitude toward the individual in Russia will come slowly and gradually and I am satisfied that we should not delay our approach to Russia in the matter of the atomic bomb until that process has been completed. My reasons are set forth in the memorandum I am handing you today. Furthermore, I believe that this long process of change in Russia is more likely to be expedited by the closer relationship in the matter of the atomic bomb which I suggest and the trust and confidence that I believe would be inspired by the method of approach which I have outlined.

MEMORANDUM BY THE SECRETARY OF WAR TO
PRESIDENT TRUMAN

Subject: Proposed Action for Control of Atomic Bombs

The advent of the atomic bomb has stimulated great military and probably even greater political interest throughout the civilized world. In a world atmosphere already extremely sensitive to power, the introduction of this weapon has profoundly affected political considerations in all sections of the globe.

In many quarters it has been interpreted as a substantial offset to the growth of Russian influence on the [European] continent. We can be certain that the Soviet government has sensed this tendency and the temptation will be strong for the Soviet political and military leaders to acquire this weapon in the shortest possible time. Britain in effect already has the status of a partner with us in the development of this weapon. Accordingly, unless the Soviets are voluntarily invited into the partnership upon a basis of cooperation and trust, we are going to maintain the Anglo-Saxon bloc over against the Soviet in the possession of this weapon. Such a condition will almost certainly stimulate feverish activity on the part of the Soviet toward the development of this bomb in what will in effect be a secret armament race of a rather desperate character. There is evidence to indicate that such activity may have already commenced. . . .

To put the matter concisely, I consider the problem of our satisfactory relations with Russia as not merely connected with but as virtually dominated by the problem of the atomic bomb. Except for the problem of the control of that bomb, those relations, while vitally important, might not be immediately pressing. The establishment of relations of mutual confidence between her and us could afford to await the slow progress of time. But with the discovery of the bomb, they become immediately emergent. These relations may be perhaps irretrievably embittered by the way in which we approach the solution of the bomb with Russia. For if we fail to approach them now and merely continue to negotiate with them, having this weapon rather ostentatiously on our hip, their suspicions and their distrust of our purposes and motives will increase. It will inspire them to greater efforts in an all out effort to solve the problem. If the solution is achieved in that spirit, it is much less likely that we will ever get the kind of covenant we may desperately need in the future. This risk is, I believe, greater than the other, inasmuch as our objective must be to get the best kind of international bargain we can—one that has some chance of being kept and saving civilization not for five or for twenty years, but forever.

The chief lesson I have learned in a long life is that the only way you can make a man trustworthy is to trust him; and the surest way to make him untrustworthy is to distrust him and show your distrust.

If the atomic bomb were merely another though more devastating military weapon to be assimilated into our pattern of international relations, it would be one thing. We could then follow the old custom of secrecy and nationalistic military superiority relying on international caution to prescribe [proscribe?] the future use of the weapon as we did with gas. But I think the bomb instead constitutes merely a first step in a new control by man over the forces of nature too revolutionary and dangerous to fit into the old concepts. I think it really caps the climax of the race between man's growing technical power for destructiveness and his psychological power of self-control and group control—his moral power. If so, our method of approach to the Russians is a question of the most vital importance in the evolution of human progress.

Since the crux of the problem is Russia, any contemplated action leading to the control of this weapon should be primarily directed *to* Russia. It is my judgment that the Soviet would be more apt to respond sincerely to a direct and forthright approach made by the United States on this subject than would be the case if the approach were made as a part of a general international scheme, or if the approach were made after a succession of express or implied threats or near threats in our peace negotiations.

My idea of an approach to the Soviets would be a direct proposal after discussion with the British that we would be prepared in effect to enter an arrangement with the Russians, the general purpose of which would be to control and limit the use of the atomic bomb as an instrument of war and so far as possible to direct and encourage the development of atomic power for peaceful and humanitarian purposes. Such an approach might more specifically lead to the proposal that we would stop work on the further improvement in, or manufacture of, the bomb as a military weapon, provided the Russians and the British would agree to do likewise. It might also provide that we would be willing to impound what bombs we now have in the United States provided the Russians and the British would agree with us that in no event will they or we use a bomb as an instrument of war unless all three Governments agree to that use. We might also consider including in the arrangement a covenant with the U.K. [United Kingdom] and the Soviets providing for the exchange of benefits of future developments whereby atomic energy may be applied on a mutually satisfactory basis for commercial or humanitarian purposes.

I would make such an approach just as soon as our immediate political considerations make it appropriate.

I emphasize perhaps beyond all other considerations the importance of taking this action with Russia as a proposal of the United States—backed by Great Britain—but peculiarly the proposal of the United States. Action of any international group of nations, including many small nations who have not demonstrated their potential power or responsibility in this war would not, in my opinion, be taken seriously by the Soviets. . . .

17   FROM   *Harry S. Truman*
The Foreign Policy of the United States
(October 27, 1945)

Stimson's advice of September 11, 1945 was not followed. At a Navy Day speech in New York City, President Truman analyzed the necessary course of American foreign policy. Its meaning for United States policy in regard to Eastern Europe and the control of the atomic bomb was direct. In what specific areas does the President's speech go beyond the principles of the Atlantic Charter?

. . . The fleet, on V-J Day, consisted of 1,200 warships, more than 50,000 supporting and landing craft, and over 40,000 navy planes. By that day, ours was a sea power never before equaled in the history of the world. . . . Now we are in the process of demobilizing our naval force. We are laying up ships. We are breaking up aircraft squadrons. We are rolling up bases and releasing officers and men. But when our demobilization is all finished as planned, the United States will still be the greatest naval power on earth.

In addition to that naval power, we shall still have one of the most powerful air forces in the world. And just the other day, so that on short notice we could mobilize a powerful and well-equipped land, sea, and air force, I asked the Congress to adopt universal training.

Why do we seek to preserve this powerful naval and air force, and establish this strong Army reserve? Why do we need them? We have assured the world time and again   and I repeat it now   that we do not seek for ourselves one inch of territory in any place in the world. Outside of the right to establish necessary bases for our own protection, we look for nothing which belongs to any other power.

We do need this kind of armed might however, and for four principal tasks: First, our Army, Navy, and Air Force, in collaboration with our Allies, must enforce the terms of peace imposed upon our defeated enemies. Second, we must fulfil the military obligations which we are undertaking as a member of the United Nations Organization—to support a lasting peace, by force if necessary. Third, we must cooperate with other American nations to preserve the territorial

SOURCE. *Department of State Bulletin*, **XIII**, October 28, 1945, pp. 653–656.

integrity and the political independence of the nations of the Western Hemisphere. Fourth, in this troubled and uncertain world, our military forces must be adequate to discharge the fundamental mission laid upon them by the Constitution of the United States—to "provide for the common defense" of the United States.

These four military tasks are directed not toward war—not toward conquest—but toward peace. We seek to use our military strength solely to preserve the peace of the world. For we now know that that is the only sure way to make our own freedom secure. . . . Let me restate the fundamentals of that foreign policy of the United States:

1. We seek no territorial expansion or selfish advantage. We have no plans for aggression against any other state, large or small. We have no objective which need clash with the peaceful aims of any other nation.

2. We believe in the eventual return of sovereign rights and self-government to all peoples who have been deprived of them by force.

3. We shall approve no territorial changes in any friendly part of the world unless they accord with the freely expressed wishes of the people concerned.

4. We believe that all peoples who are prepared for self-government should be permitted to choose their own form of government by their own freely expressed choice, without interference from any foreign source. That is true in Europe, in Asia, in Africa, as well as in the Western Hemisphere.

5. By the combined and cooperative action of our Allies, we shall help the defeated enemy states establish peaceful, democratic governments of their own free choice. And we shall try to attain a world in which Nazism, Fascism, and military aggression cannot exist.

6. We shall refuse to recognize any government imposed upon any nation by the force of any foreign power. In some cases it may be impossible to prevent forceful imposition of such a government. But the United States will not recognize any such government.

7. We believe that all nations should have the freedom of the seas and equal rights to the navigation of boundary rivers and waterways and of rivers and waterways which pass through more than one country.

8. We believe that all states which are accepted in the society of nations should have access on equal terms to the trade and the raw materials of the world.

9. We believe that the sovereign states of the Western Hemisphere,

without interference from outside the Western Hemisphere, must work together as good neighbors in the solution of their common problems.

10. We believe that full economic collaboration between all nations, great and small, is essential to the improvement of living conditions all over the world, and to the establishment of freedom from fear and freedom from want.

11. We shall continue to strive to promote freedom of expression and freedom of religion throughout the peace-loving areas of the world.

12. We are convinced that the preservation of peace between nations requires a United Nations Organization composed of all the peace-loving nations of the world who are willing jointly to use force if necessary to insure peace.

That is the foreign policy which guides the United States now. That is the foreign policy with which it confidently faces the future. It may not be put into effect tomorrow or the next day. But none the less, it is our policy; and we shall seek to achieve it. It may take a long time, but it is worth waiting for, and it is worth striving to attain. The Ten Commandments themselves have not yet been universally achieved over these thousands of years. Yet we struggle constantly to achieve them, and in many ways we come closer to them each year. Though we may meet set-backs from time to time, we shall not relent in our efforts to bring the Golden Rule into the international affairs of the world. . . .

The atomic bombs that fell on Hiroshima and Nagasaki must be made a signal, not for the old process of falling apart but for a new era—an era of ever closer unity and ever closer friendship among peaceful nations. . . . There has been talk about the atomic bomb scrapping all navies, armies, and air forces. For the present, I think that such talk is 100 percent wrong. Today control of the seas rests in the fleets of the United States and her Allies. There is no substitute for them. We have learned the bitter lesson that the weakness of this great Republic invites men of ill-will to shake the very foundations of civilization all over the world. . . .

The atomic bomb does not alter the basic foreign policy of the United States. It makes the development and application of our policy more urgent than we could have dreamed six months ago. It means that we must be prepared to approach international problems with greater speed, with greater determination, and with greater ingenuity, in order to meet a situation for which there is no precedent. . . .

As I said in my message to the Congress, discussion of the atomic bomb with Great Britain and Canada and later with other nations cannot wait upon the formal organization of the United Nations. These discussions, looking toward a free exchange of fundamental scientific information, will be begun in the near future. But I emphasize again, as I have before, that these discussions will not be concerned with the processes of manufacturing the atomic bomb or any other instruments of war.

In our possession of this weapon, as in our possession of other new weapons, there is no threat to any nation. The world, which has seen the United States in two great recent wars, knows that full well. The possession in our hands of this new power of destruction we regard as a sacred trust. Because of our love of peace, the thoughtful people of the world know that the trust will not be violated, that it will be faithfully executed.

18   FROM   *Bernard Baruch*
The United States' Plan for Controlling
(June 14, 1946) Atomic Energy

With one major exception, Russian-American relations remained deadlocked through the winter of 1945–1946. That exception, however, was the life-or-death question of controlling atomic energy. On December 27, 1945, Secretary of State Byrnes and Foreign Minister Molotov agreed to establish an Atomic Energy Commission within the United Nations. A month later, the U.N. Commission asked for specific proposals that it might consider. In March, 1946, the Truman Administration produced the Acheson-Lilienthal proposal, which recommended that the nations move through a series of stages to ultimate U.N. control of atomic weapons. The United States, in this proposal, would retain its atomic monopoly until the final stage of U.N. control would be reached. Truman then appointed Bernard Baruch as the American delegate to the U.N. Atomic Energy Commission. The Wall Street financier-Presidential advisor proceeded to rewrite key sections of the Acheson-Lilienthal report. Most important, Baruch convinced Truman that the power to veto inspections or sanctions in atomic energy matters must be destroyed. In reality, this recommendation would establish a majority rule placing preeminent power in American hands. Baruch also insisted on control of peaceful atomic energy and access to national territory (such as behind

SOURCE. U.S. *Dept. of State Bulletin,* **XIV** (June 23, 1946), pp. 1057–1062.

the Iron Curtain). His plan was unveiled as American policy at the United Nations on June 14, 1946. Five days later, Andrei Gromyko, the Soviet delegate to the U.N. Atomic Energy Commission, replied that the Baruch Plan was unacceptable for the following reasons.

1. It gave an international authority power over a nation's development of peaceful atomic energy as well as over the development of atomic weapons.

2. It allowed the United States to retain its atomic monopoly (Gromyko proposed the destruction of present atomic weapons three months after merely agreeing on a plan of control).

3. Most important, it attempted to undermine the Soviet veto in the Security Council.

With this deadlock, the last hope for international control of atomic and nuclear weapons disappeared.

What is the significance of Baruch's insistence on "access," as well as doing away with the U.N. veto on atomic energy matters, for overall American policies toward the Soviet Union?

We are here to make a choice between the quick and the dead. That is our business.

Behind the black portent of the new atomic age lies a hope which, seized upon with faith, can work our salvation. If we fail, then we have damned every man to be the slave of Fear. Let us not deceive ourselves: We must elect World Peace or World Destruction. . . .

The United States proposes the creation of an International Atomic Development Authority, to which should be entrusted all phases of the development and use of atomic energy, starting with the raw material and including

1. Managerial control or ownership of all atomic-energy activities potentially dangerous to world security.

2. Power to control, inspect, and license all other atomic activities.

3. The duty of fostering the beneficial uses of atomic energy.

4. Research and development responsibilities of an affirmative character intended to put the Authority in the forefront of atomic knowledge. . . .

When an adequate system for control of atomic energy, including the renunciation of the bomb as a weapon, has been agreed upon and put into effective operation and condign punishments set up for violations of the rules of control which are to be stigmatized as international crimes, we propose that

1. Manufacture of atomic bombs shall stop;
2. Existing bombs shall be disposed of pursuant to the terms of the treaty; and
3. The Authority shall be in possession of full information as to the know-how for the production of atomic energy. . . .

Now as to violations: in the agreement, penalties of as serious a nature as the nations may wish and as immediate and certain in their execution as possible should be fixed for

1. Illegal possession or use of an atomic bomb;
2. Illegal possession, or separation, of atomic material suitable for use in an atomic bomb;
3. Seizure of any plant or other property belonging to or licensed by the Authority;
4. Wilful interference with the activities of the Authority;
5. Creation or operation of dangerous projects in a manner contrary to, or in the absence of, a license granted by the international control body.

It would be a deception, to which I am unwilling to lend myself, were I not to say to you and to our peoples that the matter of punishment lies at the very heart of our present security system. It might as well be admitted, here and now, that the subject goes straight to the veto power contained in the Charter of the United Nations so far as it relates to the field of atomic energy. The Charter permits penalization only by concurrence of each of the five great powers—the Union of Soviet Socialist Republics, the United Kingdom, China, France, and the United States.

I want to make very plain that I am concerned here with the veto power only as it affects this particular problem. There must be no veto to protect those who violate their solemn agreements not to develop or use atomic energy for destructive purposes. . . .

I now submit the following measures as representing the fundamental features of a plan which would give effect to certain of the conclusions which I have epitomized.

General.   The Authority should set up a thorough plan for control of the field of atomic energy. . . . After this is provided for, there should be as little interference as may be with the economic plans and the present private, corporate, and state relationships in the several countries involved.

Raw Materials. The Authority should have as one of its earliest purposes to obtain and maintain complete and accurate information on world supplies of uranium and thorium and to bring them under its dominion. . . . Only after all current information on world sources of uranium and thorium is known to us all can equitable plans be made for their production, refining, and distribution.

Primary Production Plants. The Authority should exercise complete managerial control of the production of fissionable materials. This means that it should control and operate all plants producing fissionable materials in dangerous quantities and must own and control the product of these plants.

Atomic Explosives. The Authority should be given sole and exclusive right to conduct research in the field of atomic explosives. . . .

Non-Dangerous Activities. A function of the Authority should be promotion of the peace-time benefits of atomic energy. Atomic research (except in explosives), the use of research reactors, the production of radio-active tracers by means of non-dangerous reactors, the use of such tracers, and to some extent the production of power should be open to nations and their citizens under reasonable licensing arrangements from the Authority. . . .

Freedom of Access. Adequate ingress and egress for all qualified representatives of the Authority must be assured. Many of the inspection activities of the Authority should grow out of, and be incidental to, its other functions. Important measures of inspection will be associated with the tight control of raw materials, for this is a keystone of the plan. . . .

Progress by Stages. A primary step in the creation of the system of control is the setting forth, in comprehensive terms, of the functions, responsibilities, powers, and limitations of the Authority. Once a charter for the Authority has been adopted, the Authority and the system of control for which it will be responsible will require time to become fully organized and effective. The plan of control will, therefore, have to come into effect in successive stages. . . .

Disclosures. In the deliberations of the United Nations Commission on Atomic Energy, the United States is prepared to make available the information essential to a reasonable understanding of the proposals which it advocates. . . . As the successive stages of international control are reached, the United States will be prepared to yield, to the extent required by each stage, national control of activities in this field to the Authority.

CHAPTER III
RESTRUCTURING THE BRITISH EMPIRE

19   FROM   *Secretary of the Treasury Fred M.*
Vinson and Acting Secretary of State Dean Acheson:
The British Loan Agreement is Necessary for Both
American and World Prosperity (January 12, 1946)

By late 1945 the United States had failed to dislodge the developing Soviet sphere of influence in Eastern Europe. That other great exclusive bloc, the British Empire, was another matter of concern to Washington officials, and in this realm they enjoyed much greater success. Unlike Russia, Great Britain had few effective counters to meet American demands for the <u>*disestablishment of its empire*</u>*. The war had devastated the British economy. Compared with the immediate prewar years, in 1945 Great Britain's exports had declined nearly forty percent, her imports had increased more than one-third, and her overseas debt had multiplied five times. In destroying Hitler, the English had also decimated their economy both at home and abroad. Only the United States held adequate resources to rebuild the British industries and trade. Washington was willing to grant a massive loan, but in return was determined to exact the price of opening the British imperial markets to all on nearly equal terms. The following selection, the transcript of an NBC radio broadcast by the Secretary of the Treasury and the Acting Secretary of State, analyzes the loan. Which of the various reasons given for extending the loan seems most important to American policy makers?*

    This is the fifth in a group of State Department programs broadcast by the NBC University of the Air as part of a larger series entitled "Our Foreign Policy." This time the Secretary of the

SOURCE. *Department of State Bulletin*, **XIV**, January 20, 1946, pp. 51–56.

Treasury, Fred M. Vinson, and the Acting Secretary of State, Dean Acheson, will discuss "The British Loan". Sterling Fisher, Director of the NBC University of the Air, will serve as chairman of the discussion. Mr. Fisher. . . .

Fisher: The proposed loan to Great Britain has been the subject of lively discussion since its terms were announced last month. Many questions have been raised by the press and public about the loan, and it has seemed to us that they deserve frank answers. Secretary Vinson, I'd like to ask you, as one of the Americans who negotiated the agreement, to describe briefly the proposed terms. . . .

Vinson: The outlines of the agreement are simple, Mr. Fisher. We agree to advance a line of credit of $3,750,000,000 to Great Britain to buy the goods she needs from abroad to help maintain her economy while she gets back on her feet. Payment of principal and interest—the interest rate is 2 percent—start in 1951 and continue for 50 years, until the loan is paid up. The British, for their part, agree to remove many of the discriminatory exchange and import restrictions which now exist. Without the loan it would be impossible for them to do this. . . .

Fisher: I have here what is perhaps the finest collection of tough questions about the loan that has yet been made up. . . . Secretary Vinson, we might start with the question of whether Great Britain really needs a loan the size of this one.

Vinson: . . . The fact is, we went into the subject of Britain's economic condition very thoroughly, and here's where we came out—for the next few years Britain will be short several billion dollars which she needs to buy essential imports. . . .

Fisher: Why do the British find themselves in such an unfavorable spot? Haven't they looked after British interests pretty well, even during the war?

Vinson: No—the war and war production have always come first. So many British industries have been making war materials that now they have very few civilian goods to export. But even though their exports are low, the British must import huge quantities of food and raw materials in order to live. On top of all this, they have been forced to sell about four and a half billion dollars in foreign investments to keep the war going. That cut their income further. And although we supplied a lot of Britain's war needs through lend-lease, she will be in debt at the end of this year to the tune of about 14 billion dollars to her Dominions, India, and other countries. She has to export goods not only to pay for her imports but also to pay off part of that debt. And she is not yet able to produce many goods for export. . . .

Fisher: What would have happened, Mr. Vinson, if the loan negotiations had fallen through?

Vinson: The British could have existed by cutting their imports and their living standards. They would have cut their purchases from the United States, and other countries, to the very bone. This they would have had to do indefinitely and it would have meant very bad business for us. [Before the war, almost one sixth of our exports went to the United Kingdom alone, to say nothing of the Dominions.] In fact, we sold the British much more than we bought from them. We want to revive and increase that trade. But that isn't all. I'd like to point out that we're dealing here with a problem of vast dimensions. Before the war there were two great currencies in international trade—the dollar and the pound sterling. In 1938 half of the world's trade was done in these two currencies.

US needc
Br. business

Acheson: And we could add that, now that Germany and Japan are pretty well out of the picture, something like three quarters of the world's trade will be carried on in pounds and dollars. So it's not only our trade with Britain or her trade with us that is involved here.

Vinson: If both the dollar and the pound are strong, it will mean that trade everywhere will be free of excessive restrictions. The level of trade for virtually the whole world depends on the elimination of restrictions on the dollar and the pound. . . .

strong
$ + £
needed

Fisher: Mr. Acheson, what specific advantages will we reap. . . ?

Acheson: First, as soon as Congress approves the credit, the British are required to put an end to exchange controls on day-to-day business transactions with Americans. It will mean that an American manufacturer who has sold goods to Great Britain will be able to collect his proceeds in dollars.

Fisher: And after that?

Establishment of
Dollar as chief currency

Acheson: Second, at the end of one year, it is required that exchange controls be ended throughout the whole sterling area.

Fisher: Will you explain just what the sterling area is. . . ?

Acheson: The sterling area is the area where the British pound sterling is most extensively used for international transactions. It takes in the British Empire and all the Dominions, except Canada and Newfoundland, and it includes India, Egypt, Iraq, and Iceland. But I should add that under the terms of the agreement, at the end of a year no restrictions will be imposed by the British on day-to-day transactions in *any* part of the world. . . .

Fisher: And about imperial preference, Mr. Acheson—the system whereby Britain gives tariff preference to British Empire goods as compared to American goods.

Acheson: The British have agreed to support the American proposals to reduce and eventually eliminate these special privileges. In some ways, the joint American and British statement on commercial policy is the most important part of the agreement. The United States has made certain proposals for consideration by a United Nations trade conference, which we expect will be held late next summer. The British have joined us in these proposals for tariff reductions and an end to hampering restrictions of all sorts.

Fisher: Now, Mr. Acheson, what bearing does Britain's war record have on the loan?

Acheson: Mr. Fisher, all of us have great admiration for the British and we think they did a great job in the war. We have great sympathy for what they have suffered. But that has nothing to do with this loan. This loan is not a pension for a worthy war partner. It's not a handout. It's not a question of relief, of bundles for Britain. This loan looks to the future, not to the past. It does the things that are necessary to keep the kind of world we want. We're willing to bet three and three-quarters billion dollars that we and the British can make it work. . . .

Fisher: The advantages do add up to quite a lot. . . .

Acheson: If all the interest payments are met, Britain will eventually pay us back $2,200,000,000 more than the credit we're advancing. That's a very considerable sum. . . .

Fisher: Then there's this question, Mr. Vinson. . . . In helping Britain to get back on her feet, won't we be financing our competitor? Won't this endanger American trade, in the long run?

Vinson: That notion is based on a fallacy—the mistaken idea that there is only so much trade to be had—the idea that foreign trade is like a melon, and if someone else gets a big slice you get a smaller one, in direct proportion. That's simply not true. As trade increases, there is more for everybody. And the principal purpose of this loan is to increase international trade generally.

Acheson: It isn't *competitive* trade that we fear, it's *discriminatory* trade—trade hampered by high tariffs, exchange restrictions, quotas and so on. The British loan enables us to move away from these devices, which limit our ability to sell abroad.

Vinson: And let's not forget the fact that Britain is normally our best overseas customer. She can buy more abroad only if she is prosperous, and if she sells more abroad. . . .

Fisher: What is the alternative?

Acheson: The alternative is that we do not get the commercial arrangements which are necessary for the survival of our free industrial system. The alternative is the division of the world into warring economic blocs.

Fisher: Do you agree with that dire prediction, Mr. Vinson?

Vinson: Yes, Dean is absolutely right. The alternative to helping the British is to face an extension and tightening up of the whole series of trade and exchange controls that have been put in effect during the war. The world would soon be divided into a few relatively closed economic regions. That would mean restricted trade, lower living standards, bitter rivalry, and stored-up hatred for the United States as the richest nation in the world. That would be a dangerous course to take. I'm confident that we'll have sense enough to choose the other way.

Fisher: To summarize what you've said, then, the proposed British loan is an essential step toward the expanding world trade that we need if we are to remain prosperous. . . .

20   FROM   *R. J. G. Boothby in*
                House of Commons Debate: Attack on Loan
          Do Not Sell the British Empire for a
     Packet of Cigarettes (December 12, 1945)

Most British spokesmen did not share the sanguine view of the loan held by Dean Acheson and other American officials. The British government had initially hoped for a larger, interest-free loan. That these points had not been gained was disquieting, but when the United States further demanded an end to the exclusivity of their economic privileges within the Empire, many Englishmen were shocked and angered. The loan had been negotiated by the Labour Government of Clement Attlee, who had replaced Churchill as the British leader in the national elections held in July 1945. Churchill, now the leader of the minority opposition in the House, sadly abstained from voting on the loan agreement. Some of his Conservative Party colleagues were not as restrained. One of the bitterest attacks was made by R. J. G. Boothby of the Conservatives. Many

SOURCE. *Parliamentary Debates*, Fifth Series, Volume 417, House of Commons, December 12, 1945, pp. 455–469.

of Boothby's arguments were notable, particularly his accurate prophesy that the British would not be able to rebuild their economy sufficiently while repaying the loan; his attack on a "frontier thesis," which he believed underlay the American faith in a multilateral, liberal economy; and his warning that the policy would lead to a world "divided into two . . . opposing systems." He was incorrect in believing the United States would suffer from a major postwar depression, although many officials in both London and Washington shared his fear. Do the statements of Clayton, Acheson, Vinson, and other American leaders in this volume confirm Boothby's characterization of United States policy as resting on "free, knock-about Capitalism"?

. . . I conscientiously believe that this country is not, and will not be, in a position to discharge the obligation she is being invited to undertake by the Government. . . . I have never believed that you can get out of debt by getting into more debt; and I do not think this is going to make our position any stronger.

We spent £10,700 million over and above what we could provide ourselves on the war; and of this sum £9,200 million was spent during the war, leaving us on "V-J Day" with another £1,500 million of inevitable war expenditure to be paid. . . . This extra £1,500 million should have been included in Lend-Lease. It was essential war expenditure. . . . Lend-Lease was passed in the United States as an "Act for the defence of the United States." That is exactly what it was, comparable precisely to the subsidies we ourselves paid to various European countries during the Napoleonic Wars, with great success, when we wanted them to fight our battles for us.

Unlike the last war which was officially terminated by Presidential proclamation on 2nd July, 1921, this one came to an end within three weeks of the termination of hostilities. I can see no justification for this. It was like giving a man a lift in an aeroplane, as Mr. Roosevelt gave us under Lend-Lease, taking him nine-tenths of the way across the Atlantic Ocean, and then, when 200 miles from the shore, throwing him out of the aeroplane and telling him to swim for it. . . .

I estimate that the cost of amortization of the sterling balances in dollars plus the cost of the American Loan, will come to just over £100,000,000 a year; and that is a burden which, I say, this country will not, in any forseeable future, be able to sustain. It is an obligation we shall not be able to meet. It represents about 10 percent of our present target for exports and over 20 percent of our pre-war exports; and it is about half as heavy . . . as the burden of reparations imposed on Germany after the last war, by the Dawes Plan. I do not really see that our war performance during the past six years has called for the imposition of such a burden. . . .

As I have already said, in order to obtain the necessary imports to pay our debts, we shall have to increase our exports by 75 percent a year. . . .

Under the Bretton Woods Agreement, gold will purchase any currency. . . . Of 28 billion dollars of monetary gold in the world, 23 billion are in the vaults of Fort Knox. If we are going to make gold the basis of credit, in my estimation, we are handing over world economic power, outside the Soviet Union, finally and decisively to the United States. . . .

Boothby realizes loss of £ pounds power

The third condition that we are now asked to swallow is the acceptance of the principle of non-discrimination in trade, involving the elimination of imperial preference and of quotas on imports. I do not think there is any need for me to dilate on this. I think if it is persisted in—and I hope it will not be—it will involve the break-up of the British Empire. . . . Nearly half our exports before the war went to the British Empire. . . .

Is there anything in the Agreement which obliges the United States of America, in any circumstances, to make cuts in her tariffs of a magnitude which would ensure a substantial importation of goods into the United States of America? Anyway, what is the value of the United States of America as a market to this country? Compare it with the value of the Empire market, which we are throwing away. . . .

I am going to speak bluntly, and say that there are two main objectives underlying the agreement which we are being asked to approve. The first is to get back as quickly as possible to the economic system of the 19th century①—the system of *laissez faire* capitalism. The second is to break up, and prise open②the markets of the world for the benefit of the United States of America, who have an intense desire to get rid of their surplus products, which will be enormous, at almost any cost. . . .

2 aims of B

I want now to put two propositions to the Chancellor of the Exchequer. The first is that multilateral trade and free convertibility, to which this Agreement admittedly commits us, are impractical in the modern world. . . . The philosophy underlying the old Liberal doctrine of enlightened self-interest and the free-market economy depended for its success on the existence of empty spaces and continually expanding markets. The spaces are filling up. The era of uncontrolled capitalist expansion is drawing to a close. I never thought I should live to teach these things to hon. Members [the

Labour Party] who sit on the Government side of the House. The *laissez faire* economy of the 19th century, I would remind the Chancellor of the Exchequer, who used to think this himself, has now to give way to the planned economy of the 20th century.

My second proposition is that we cannot have a planned national economy with international economic anarchy. It has been left to a Socialist Government [the Labour Government] to lead us back to international economic anarchy and to the economic system of the 19th century, the system of *laissez faire* capitalism, which crashed to destruction in 1929. The next time that an American slump comes— will anybody deny, by the way, the possibility of another American slump? Or do we all think that America's economic stability is now so great that they will never have another. . . ? It is great optimism on their part if they place such reliance in the operation of free, knock-about Capitalism. I have no such confidence in the economic system of the United States of America. I think there may quite possibly be a slump there. And if there is, His Majesty's Government are, by these measures, depriving us of every weapon by which we might protect ourselves from its most dire consequences. . . .

There was a great chance, for a middle unit, standing between what . . . I call the knock-about Capitalism of the United States of America on the one hand, and the rigid, Socialist, closed economy of Russia on the other; free to expand, by multilateral agreement within that economy, between like-minded nations. That arrangement might have provided a balancing *bloc* which would have been of very great value in the world. I do not want to see the world divided into two, and only two, opposing systems. I think there is great danger in it.

. . . I never thought I should feel again as I felt at the time of the Munich Agreement, but I feel just the same as I did then. This is our economic Munich. . . . I would not venture to dogmatize. But there is one mandate which his Majesty's Government never got from the people of this country, and that was to sell the British Empire for a packet of cigarettes.

CHAPTER IV
POLAND, THE SYMBOL

21 FROM   *U.S. Department of State:*
Why the United States is Interested in
Poland (Not dated, but probably December
1944–January 1945)

Until the close of the war when the problem of reconstructing Germany arose, no specific issue more endangered Soviet-American relations and the course of the postwar peace than did the question of Poland. Russia and Poland had long been unfriendly; twice in a single lifetime Poland had served as the avenue for German invasions of Russia. The Soviets were determined to seal off that avenue, despite American opposition to anything resembling a Soviet-imposed government in Warsaw. After Poland had been divided between Germany and Russia in 1939–1940, a Polish government-in-exile established itself in London. An opposition group began operating out of Moscow. Churchill and Roosevelt supported the London regime, although never to the point of insisting that Stalin recognize that group as the sole, legitimate Polish government in London had evidence that this massacre had been committed by Soviet troops a Russo-Polish boundary which would be advantageous to the Soviets. In 1943 a mass grave of 10,000 Polish officers was found in the Katyn Forest. The Polish government in London had evidence that this massacre had been commited by Soviet troops in 1940. Stalin indignantly denied this charge, and proceeded to use the ensuing exchange of protests as an excuse to break relations with the London government-in-exile. When Soviet troops swept across Poland in 1944, the supposed Russian assault on Warsaw was accompanied by a mass uprising within the city of the Polish underground, many of whose leaders were sympathetic to the London group. Instead of moving into Warsaw, however, the Russian troops remained outside the city while German armies destroyed the uprising. Stalin gave sound military reasons for halting the advance outside the city, but the United States and Great Britain believed that the Soviets stopped for

SOURCE. U.S. Dept. of State, *Foreign Relations of the United States; The Conferences at Malta and Yalta, 1945* (Washington, D.C.: 1955), pp. 235–236.

political as well as military reasons, particularly after Stalin summarily rejected Churchill's and Roosevelt's pleas that American and British pilots be at least allowed to drop supplies to the underground. By the eve of the Yalta Conference, scheduled for February 1945, Stalin had installed the Moscow Poles in power at Warsaw. Poland was sinking rapidly behind an iron curtain. American officials understood, even if they did not completely agree with, Russian political moves in Poland. But they did not accept the accompanying economic policies. The following selection is a Briefing Book Paper prepared by the Department of State for President Roosevelt's use at Yalta. A series of these papers was prepared on the principal topics that would be discussed by the President at Yalta. What connection does the State Department see between economic and political events in Poland?

---

1. INTERESTS OF THE UNITED STATES

Economic

a. Interest in the early return of trade to a multilateral basis under the freest possible conditions. The pattern of Europe's future commercial policy will be strongly influenced, if not largely determined, by policies and procedures established during the period of reconstruction. Whether postwar conditions lead back to bilateralism, restriction and autarchy, or are resolved in a manner which will permit the progressive growth and liberalization of trade and investment will depend in no small measure on the ability of the wartorn countries to obtain outside (i.e., mostly American) help in reconstruction.

b. Interest in general European economic stability. This stability depends on the maintenance of sound economic conditions and reasonable prosperity in all parts of the Continent.

Political. It now seems clear that the Soviet Union will exert predominant political influence over the areas in question [Poland and the Balkans]. While this Government probably would not want to oppose itself to such a political configuration, neither would it desire to see American influence in this part of the world completely nullified.

In the situation which is likely to prevail in Poland and the Balkan states after the war, the United States can hope to make its influence felt only if some degree of equal opportunity in trade, investment, and access to sources of information is preserved. American aid in the reconstruction of these areas would not only gain the good-will of the populations involved, but would also help bring about conditions which would permit the adoption of relatively liberal policies of this nature.

2. TYPES OF RECONSTRUCTION NEEDS

The reconstruction needs of the areas under reference will, of course, vary from country to country. Poland is the only country that may require extensive industrial reconstruction. . . .

3. POSSIBLE FORMS OF AMERICAN PARTICIPATION

The United States can share in the reconstruction of Poland and the Balkans in several different ways, prominent among which would be direct loans from the Export-Import Bank and participation in loans by the International Bank for Reconstruction and Development. Private American investment is unlikely in this area for some years to come at least.

loans

Probably one of the most useful and at the same time least expensive forms in which the United States can aid in the reconstruction of Poland and the Balkan states is by making available to them technical assistance, especially in the field of agriculture.

technical aid

4. THE SOVIET ATTITUDE TOWARD UNITED STATES PARTICIPATION

The attitude of the Soviet Union toward American participation in the reconstruction of Poland and the Balkans is uncertain. It seems clear that, for security reasons, the Soviet Government is seeking to make sure that these countries will be oriented to the East both politically and economically.

However, in the case of one or another of the border countries, Poland, for example, the Russians might have grounds to feel at an early date that an Eastern political orientation was more or less assured in any case and that foreign loans to such countries could have no decisive influence in this respect. Furthermore, the Soviet Union will have some interest in seeing that her neighbors prosper under her tutelage.

The Soviet Union probably would like most to borrow herself the money that might be available for the border countries, and to finance from the resources available to her their reconstruction and development needs. The Soviet Union might prefer, in any case, to have the reconstruction and development of the border countries financed through the International Bank rather than through direct loans from the United States.

22   FROM   *Churchill, Roosevelt,*
Stalin at Yalta:

Caesar's Wife in Fact Had Her Sins
(February 6−11, 1945)

At Yalta, the problem of Poland was thoroughly discussed by the Big Three. As the following selection reveals, Stalin announced clearly that the Soviets put highest priority on Polish affairs; although the British viewed the question as a matter of "honor," for Russia it was a question both of "honor and security." Stalin insisted on the Curzon line as the Polish-Russian boundary. This demarcation gave Russia parts of Poland as it existed in 1939, and was the issue on which the Russians had become most annoyed with the Polish government-in-exile in London. In turn, Stalin suggested moving the Polish western boundary further westward at the expense of Germany. The "crucial point of this great conference," as Churchill stated, was reached when the Big Three began discussing the composition of a Polish government. The result of these discussions was announced on February 11; notice particularly in this announcement the phrase that the government then functioning in Poland "should therefore be re-organized on a broader democratic basis with the inclusion of democratic leaders from Poland itself and from Poles abroad." For the next five months Churchill and Roosevelt (later Truman) argued bitterly with Stalin over the correct interpretation of these words. Given the preceding discussion in this selection, what interpretation should be given this sentence?

FEBRUARY 6, 1945

The President said that the United States was farther away from Poland than anyone else here, and that there were times when a long distance point of view was useful. He said that at Teheran he had stated that he believed the American people were in general favorably inclined to the Curzon Line as the eastern frontier of Poland, but he felt that if the Soviet Government would consider a concession in regard to Lwow and the oil deposits in the Province of Lwow that would have a very salutary effect. He said that he was merely putting forth this suggestion for consideration and would not insist on it. He said that in regard to the government he wished to see the creation

SOURCE. U. S. Dept. of State, *Foreign Relations of the United States, The Conferences at Malta and Yalta, 1945* (Washington, D.C.: 1955), pp. 667–671, 776–781, 852–854, 980.

of a representative government which could have the support of all the great powers and which could be composed of representatives of the principal parties of Poland. He said one possibility which had been suggested was the creation of a Presidential Council composed of Polish leaders which could then create a government composed of the chiefs of the five political parties—Workers Party, Peasant Party, Socialist Party, etc. He said that one thing must be made certain and that was that Poland should maintain the most friendly and co-operative relations with the Soviet Union. . . .

The Prime Minister said that he had consistently declared in Parliament and elsewhere that the British Government would support the Curzon Line, even leaving Lwow to the Soviet Union. He had been criticized for this and so had Mr. Eden, but he felt that after the burdens which Russia had borne in this war the Curzon Line was not a decision of force but one of right. . . . Of course, he added, if the mighty Soviet Union could make some gesture to the much weaker country, such as the relinquishment of Lwow, this act of magnanimity would be acclaimed and admired. He said he was much more interested in sovereignty and independence of Poland than in the frontier line—he wanted to see the Poles have a home where they could organize their lives as they wished. That was an objective that he had often heard Marshal Stalin proclaim most firmly, and he put his trust in those declarations. . . . It must not be forgotten, however, that Great Britain had gone to war to protect Poland against German aggression at a time when that decision was most risky, and it had almost cost them their life in the world. He said Great Britain had no material interest in Poland, but the question was one of honor and that his government would therefore never be content with a solution which did not leave Poland a free and independent state. The freedom of Poland, however, did not cover any hostile designs or intrigue against the U.S.S.R., and none of us should permit this. . . . He said that the British Government recognized the present Polish government in London but did not have intimate contact with it. . . . He inquired whether there might be some possibility of forming a government here for Poland which would utilize these men. . . .

At the suggestion of Marshal Stalin, there was a ten-minute intermission.

Marshal Stalin then gave the following summary of his views on the Polish question: Mr. Churchill had said that for Great Britain the Polish question was one of honor and that he understood, but for the Russians it was a question both of honor and security. It was one of honor because Russia had many past grievances against Poland and desired to see them eliminated. It was a question of strategic security not only because Poland was a bordering country but because throughout history Poland had been the corridor for attack on Russia. We have to mention that during the last thirty years Germany twice has passed through this corridor. The reason for this was that Poland was weak. Russia wants a strong, independent and democratic Poland. . . . It is not only a question of honor for Russia, but one of life and death. . . .

In regard to the Curzon Line, concessions in regard to Lwow and the Lwow Province, and Mr. Churchill's reference to a magnanimous act on our part, it is necessary to remind you that not Russians but Curzon [Lord Curzon, British Secretary of State for Foreign Affairs, 1919–1924] and Clemenceau [Georges Clemenceau, French Premier, 1917–1920] fixed this line [in 1919–1920]. The Russians had not been invited and the line was established against their will. Lenin had opposed giving Biolystok Province to the Poles but the Curzon Line gives it to Poland. We have already retreated from Lenin's position in regard to this province. Should we then be less Russian than Curzon and Clemenceau? We could not then return to Moscow and face the people who would say Stalin and Molotov have been less sure defenders of Russian interest than Curzon and Clemenceau. It is, therefore, impossible to agree with the proposed modification of the line. I would prefer to have the war go on although it will cost us blood in order to compensate for Poland from Germany. When in Moscow Mr. Mikolajczyk [leader of the Polish Government in exile in London] was delighted to hear that Poland's frontier would extend to the West Neisse River [thereby moving the Polish boundary several hundred miles into Germany] and I favor the Polish frontier on the West Neisse. . . .

As to the question of the Polish government, Mr. Churchill has said it would be good to create a Polish government here. I am afraid that was a slip of the tongue, for without participation of the Poles it is impossible to create a Polish government. . . . Last autumn in Moscow there was a good chance for a fusion of the various Polish elements and in the meeting between Mikolajczyk, Grabski [both from the London exile government] and Lublin Poles [the pro-Communist Polish government in Poland] various points of agreement were reached as Mr. Churchill will remember. Mikolajczyk left for London but did not return since he was expelled from office precisely because he wanted agreement. Arcixzewski and Raczkiewicz [both members of the Polish government in exile in London] are not only against agreement but are hostile to any idea of an agreement. Arcixzewski has characterized the Lublin Poles as bandits and criminals and they naturally pay him back in the same coin. It will be difficult to bring them together. . . . I must say that the Warsaw government [that is, the Lublin government] has a democratic base equal at least to that of de Gaulle [in France].

As a military man I demand from a country liberated by the Red Army that there be no civil war in the rear. The men in the Red Army are indifferent to the type of government as long as it will maintain order and they will not be shot in the back. The Warsaw, or Lublin, government has not badly fulfilled this task. There are, however, agents of the London government who claim to be agents of the underground forces of resistance. I must say that no good and much evil comes from these forces. Up to the present time they have killed 212 of our military men. . . . When I compare what the agents of the Lublin government have done and what the agents of the London government have done I see the first are good and the second bad. . . .

The Prime Minister said that he must put on record the fact that the British and Soviet Governments have different sources of information in Poland and therefore they obtain different views of the situation there. . . . He believed, he added, that with the best of all their information he could not feel that the Lublin government represents more than one third of the people and would be maintained in power if the people were free to express their opinion. . . . The Prime Minister said he agreed that anyone who attacks the Red Army should be punished, but he repeated that the British Government could not agree to recognizing the Lublin government of Poland.

The conference then adjourned until four o'clock tomorrow.

FEBRUARY 8, 1945

The Prime Minister said that we were now at the crucial point of this great conference. He said we would be found wanting by the world should we separate recognizing different Polish governments. . . . To break altogether with the lawful government of Poland [that is, the Polish government in exile in London] which had been recognized during all these five years of war would be an act subject to the most severe criticism in England. . . . Great Britain would be charged with forsaking the cause of Poland and he was bound to say that the debates

in Parliament would be most painful and he might add most dangerous to Allied unity. . . . He said if they were to give up the London
government it must be evident that a new start had been made on both
sides from equal terms. Before such transfer of recognition His
Majesty's Government would have to be convinced that a new government, representative of the Polish people, had been created, pledged
to an election on the basis of universal suffrage by secret ballot
with the participation of all democratic parties and the right to put
up their candidates. . . .

The President said we were all agreed on the necessity of free
elections and that the only problem was how Poland was to be
governed in the interval.

Marshal Stalin said that he had heard complaints from the Prime
Minister that he had no information in regard to the situation in
Poland. Mr. Churchill could get this information and he did not see
why Great Britain and the United States could not send their own
people into Poland. He said in regard to the popularity of the
Provisional Government [that is, the Lublin, or Warsaw govern-
ment] he could assure the conference that the people running the
government were popular. . . . He said it would be better to deal with
the reconstruction of the Provisional Government rather than to
attempt to set up a new one. He said he felt Mr. Molotov was right,
and rather than a presidential committee we might agree on increasing
the Provisional Government.

The President asked how long it would be, in the Marshal's opinion,
before elections could be held in Poland.

Marshal Stalin replied it might be possible in a month provided no
catastrophes occurred on the front and the Germans began to beat
them.

FEBRUARY 9, 1945

Prime Minister: In Parliament I must be able to say that the elections will be held in a fair way. I do not care much about Poles myself.

Stalin: There are some very good people among the Poles. They are
good fighters. Of course, they fight among themselves too. . . .

President: I want this election in Poland to be the first one beyond
question. It should be like Caesar's wife. I did not know her but they
said she was pure.

Stalin: They said that about her but in fact she had her sins. . . .

FEBRUARY 11, 1945

The following Declaration on Poland was agreed by the Conference:

"A new situation has been created in Poland as a result of her complete liberation by the Red Army. This calls for the establishment of a Polish Provisional Government which can be more broadly based than was possible before the recent liberation of the Western part of Poland. The Provisional Government which is now functioning in Poland should therefore be reorganized on a broader democratic basis with the inclusion of democratic leaders from Poland itself and from Poles abroad. This new Government should then be called the Polish Provisional Government of National Unity. . . .

This Polish Provisional Government of National Unity shall be pledged to the holding of free and unfettered elections as soon as possible on the basis of universal suffrage and secret ballot. In these elections all democratic and anti-Nazi parties shall have the right to take part and to put forward candidates. . . .

The three Heads of Government consider that the Eastern frontier of Poland should follow the Curzon Line with digressions from it in some regions of five to eight kilometres in favour of Poland. They recognize that Poland must receive substantial accessions of territory in the North and West. They feel that the opinion of the New Polish Provisional Government of National Unity should be sought in due course on the extent of these accessions and that the final delimitation of the Western frontier of Poland should thereafter await the Peace Conference."

23   FROM   *Roosevelt to Stalin*
"I Cannot Reconcile This Either with our
Agreement or Our Discussions" (April 1, 1945)

At Yalta, Churchill argued that members of the Polish government in London should be included in the Warsaw government, Roosevelt strongly urged that elections as "pure" as "Caesar's wife" be held in Poland, and Stalin indicated that he preferred the current Warsaw government which was dominated by men close to Moscow. The final announcement on reorganizing the Polish government was interpreted by the

SOURCE. U.S. Dept. of State, *Foreign Relations of the United States, 1945*, V (Washington, 1967), pp. 194–196.

Russians to mean that the pro-Moscow Poles should remain in control, although one or several London Poles might be invited to join. The Allies believed the announcement meant that the pro-Russian Polish government could be a part, but not the determinant part, of a new government. By March, discussions on the question had broken down. Churchill urged Roosevelt to protest to Stalin because if the Polish government remained intact, then, the Prime Minister warned, "how much more of Eastern Europe" would ultimately be ruled by "the Russian version of democracy?" The President wrote a strong letter to Stalin on April 1. The "Commission" referred to in the letter was established by the Big Three at Yalta to carry out the agreement on Poland. What is the significance of Roosevelt's several references to the need for "genuine popular support in the United States"?

Stalin answered Roosevelt's letter within a week. The Soviet leader was now willing to allow three Poles from London to participate in a reorganized Warsaw government; previously he had only allowed one. Stalin required, however, that these three representatives accept the new Russian-Polish boundary (the Curzon line). This reply eased the tension, but it by no means solved the problem.

PRESIDENT ROOSEVELT TO STALIN

I cannot conceal from you the concern with which I view the development of events of mutual interest since our fruitful meeting at Yalta. . . . So far there has been a discouraging lack of progress made in the carrying out, which the world expects, of the political decisions which we reached at the Conference particularly those relating to the Polish question. I am frankly puzzled as to why this should be and must tell you that I do not fully understand in many respects the apparent indifferent attitude of your Government. Having understood each other so well at Yalta I am convinced that the three of us can and will clear away any obstacles which have developed since then. I intend, therefore, in this message to lay before you with complete frankness the problem as I see it. . . .

[The] part of our agreements at Yalta which has aroused the greatest popular interest and is the most urgent relates to the Polish question. You are aware of course that the Commission which we set up has made no progress. I feel this is due to the interpretation which your Government is placing upon the Crimean decisions. . . .

In the discussions that have taken place so far your Government appears to take the position that the new Polish Provisional Government of National Unity which we agreed should be formed should be little more than a continuation of the present Warsaw Government.

I cannot reconcile this either with our agreement or our discussions. While it is true that the Lublin Government is to be reorganized and its members play a prominent role it is to be done in such a fashion as to bring into being a new Government. This point is clearly brought out in several places in the text of the agreement. I must make it quite plain to you that any such solution which would result in a thinly disguised continuance of the present Warsaw regime would be unacceptable and would cause the people of the United States to regard the Yalta agreement as having failed. It is equally apparent that for the same reason the Warsaw Government cannot under the agreement claim the right to select or reject what Poles are to be brought to Moscow by the Commission for consultation. Can we not agree that it is up to the Commission to select the Polish leaders to come to Moscow to consult in the first instance and invitations be sent out accordingly. If this could be done I see no great objection to having the Lublin group come first in order that they may be fully acquainted with the agreed interpretation of the Yalta decisions on this point. It is of course understood that if the Lublin group comes first no arrangements would be made independently with them before the arrival of the other Polish leaders called for consultation. In order to facilitate the agreement the Commission might first of all select a small but representative group of Polish leaders who could suggest other names for the consideration of the Commission. We have not and would not bar or veto any candidate for consultation which Mr. Molotov might propose being confident that he would not suggest any Poles who would be inimical to the intent of the Crimean decision. I feel that it is not too much to ask that my Ambassador be accorded the same confidence and that any candidate for consultation presented by any one of the Commission be accepted by the others in good faith. . . . While the foregoing are the immediate obstacles which in my opinion have prevented the Commission from making any progress in this vital matter there are two other suggestions which were not in the agreement but nevertheless have a very important bearing on the result we all seek. Neither of these suggestions has been as yet accepted by your Government. I refer to (1) that there should be the maximum of political tranquility in Poland and that dissident groups should cease any measures and countermeasures against each other. . . . (2) It would also seem entirely natural in view of the responsibilities placed upon them by the agreement that representatives of the American and British members of the Commission should be permitted to visit Poland. As you will recall Mr.

Molotov himself suggested this at an early meeting of the Commission and only subsequently withdrew it.

I wish I could convey to you how important it is for the successful development of our program of international collaboration that this Polish question be settled fairly and speedily. If this is not done all of the difficulties and dangers to Allied unity which we had so much in mind in reaching our decision at the Crimea will face us in an even more acute form. You are, I am sure, aware that genuine popular support in the United States is required to carry out any Government policy foreign or domestic. The American people make up their own mind and no Governmental action can change it. . . .

24 FROM *Two White House Meetings: We Are Faced with a Soviet "Barbarian Invasion of Europe" (April 20 and 23, 1945)*

Within a week after Roosevelt's funeral, President Truman summoned his top foreign policy advisers to thrash out a policy for solving East-West problems. Kept out of the policy-making circle by Roosevelt, the new President knew little about postwar planning. As a two-term Senator from Missouri, however, Truman had publicly voiced his dislike of Russia. This feeling, combined with his personal determination to be President in his own right and to exercise the powers of his office to the fullest, made Truman particularly susceptible to advisers who urged a tough stand against the Soviets. Foremost among such advisers was the American Ambassador to Russia, W. Averell Harriman. In the account of a top-level policy session of April 20 which follows, Harriman takes the lead in explaining the danger of the Soviet position on Poland. Truman merely, but significantly, interjects several times his determination to be "firm" with the Russians. What is the meaning of Truman's statements that "the Soviet Union needed us more than we needed them," and although the United States could not get 100 percent, "we should be able to get 85 percent"?

Three days later, as Truman was preparing to meet that day with Russian Foreign Minister V. M. Molotov, another strategy session was held. Again the Polish issue dominated the discussion, but this time there was an objection offered to the Administration's course. It came from Secretary of War Henry Stimson, not hitherto known

SOURCE. The April 20 meeting is recounted in U.S. Dept. of State, *Foreign Relations of the United States, Volume V, Europe* (Washington, D.C.: 1967), pp. 231–234. The account of the April 23 meeting is taken from the diary of Henry L. Stimson, April 23, 1945, Henry L. Stimson papers, Yale University Library, and reprinted by permission of the Stimson Literary Trust and Yale University Library.

for having soft views on Soviet policy. Stimson wanted to be tough, but not on Poland. His objections, however, went considerably deeper. He believed that since the United States and Russia were indisputably the two super-powers in the world, they would have to solve their common problems bilaterally before the United Nations could function effectively. His views resembled Stalin's remark to Harry Hopkins that it was rather inconceivable that on major issues Honduras and Costa Rica could have votes equal to the U.S. or the U.S.S.R. Stimson was overruled, and later, Truman proceeded to tell Molotov that the Soviets had to change their Polish policy. The President did so, moreover, in "words of one syllable." How do you assess the totality of Stimson's views, including his remarks on free ballots, in judging whether he had taken the proper stand on the Polish issue?

MEMORANDUM OF CONVERSATION AT THE WHITE HOUSE, APRIL 20, 1945

. . . At the President's request Ambassador Harriman [Ambassador to the Soviet Union W. Averell Harriman] then made a brief report on his opinion of the present problems facing the United States in relation to the Soviet Union. He said that he thought the Soviet Union had two policies which they thought they could successfully pursue at the same time—one, the policy of cooperation with the United States and Great Britain, and the other, the extension of Soviet control over neighboring states through unilateral action. He said that he thought our generosity and desire to cooperate was being misinterpreted in Moscow by certain elements around Stalin as an indication that the Soviet Government could do anything that it wished without having any trouble with the United States. He said that he thought the Soviet Government did not wish to break with the United States since they needed our help in order to reduce the burden of reconstruction and that he felt we had nothing to lose by standing firm on issues that were of real importance to us. . . . The President said that he was not in any sense afraid of the Russians and that he intended to be firm but fair since in his opinion the Soviet Union needed us more than we needed them. Ambassador Harriman said that he believed that some quarters in Moscow believed erroneously that American business needed as a matter of life and death the development of exports to Russia. Mr. Harriman said that this was of course not true but that a number of Russian officials believed it. The President again repeated that he intended to be firm with the Russians and make no concessions from American principles or traditions for the fact of winning their favor. He said he felt that only on a give and take basis could any relations be established.

Ambassador Harriman said that in effect what we were faced with was a "barbarian invasion of Europe," that Soviet control over any foreign country did not mean merely influence on their foreign relations but the extension of the Soviet system with secret police, extinction of freedom of speech, etc., and that we had to decide what should be our attitude in the face of these unpleasant facts. He added that he was not pessimistic and felt that we could arrive at a workable basis with the Russians but that this would require a reconsideration of our policy and the abandonment of the illusion that for the immediate future the Soviet Government was going to act in accordance with the principles which the rest of the world held to in international affairs. He said that obviously certain concessions in the give and take of negotiation would have to be made. The President said that he thoroughly understood this and said that we could not, of course, expect to get 100 percent of what we wanted but that on important matters he felt that we should be able to get 85 percent.

The Ambassador then outlined briefly the issues involved in the Polish question explaining his belief that Stalin had discovered from the Lublin Poles that an honest execution of the Crimean [Yalta] decision would mean the end of Soviet-backed Lublin control over Poland since any real democratic leader such as Mikolajczyk would serve as a rallying point for 80 or 90 percent of the Polish people against the Lublin Communists. . . .

He said he would like to inquire in this connection of the President how important he felt the Polish question was in relation to the San Francisco Conference [where the United Nations would be set in motion] and American participation in the world organization. The President replied immediately and decisively that in his considered opinion unless settlement of the Polish question was achieved along the lines of the Crimean decision that the treaty of American adherence to a world organization would not get through the Senate. He added that he intended to tell Molotov just this in words of one syllable. . . .

HENRY L. STIMSON'S ACCOUNT OF THE
APRIL 23, 1945 MEETING

[The President summoned Secretary of War Stimson to be at the White House at 2:00 P.M. Secretary of State Edward Stettinius, Secretary of the Navy James Forrestal, Army Chief of Staff George

Marshall, Admiral William Leahy (Chief of Staff to the President), Major General John R. Deane (Commanding General, U.S. Military Mission in the Soviet Union), and Ambassador to the Soviet Union W. Averell Harriman were among those present.]

Stettinius had gotten into a jam with Molotov . . . who arrived yesterday. The subject is Poland. The Russians have apparently flatly refused to permit the agreement at Yalta to be carried out to select a mixed delegation from Poland and they are insisting that the Lublin people shall be recognized as the government of Poland. After Stettinius had described the situation as being a flat repudiation of the agreement in the Crimea . . . [the President] described with rather brutal frankness what he was going to say to the Russians and then said he called us in to ask our advice. Well of course I had never been at Yalta and I didn't know what happened there and I was at a great disadvantage. He called on me first. And furthermore I had never felt that it was a wise thing to go ahead with the San Francisco conference without having first adjusted all the problems that might come up between us and Russia and Great Britain first. Now we are reaping the penalty for that piece of heedlessness and we are at loggerheads with Russia on an issue which in my opinion is very dangerous and one which she is not likely to yield on in substance. Furthermore, although at Yalta she apparently agreed to a free and independent ballot for the ultimate choice of the representatives of Poland, yet I know very well from my experience with other nations that there are no nations in the world except the U.S. and the U.K. [United Kingdom] which have a real idea of what an independent free ballot is. I learned that in Nicaragua and in South America, and I was very much alarmed for fear that we were rushing into a situation where we would find ourselves breaking our relations with Russia on the most important and difficult question which we and Russia have got between us.

All this was fired at me like a shot out of a Gatling gun and before I had really had time to crystallize my views at all. . . . So I held back and told the President that I was very much troubled by it and I pointed out all these difficulties that I have just spoken of. I said that in my opinion we ought to be very careful and see whether we couldn't get ironed out on the situation without getting into a headon collision. He was evidently disappointed at my caution and advice and passed along the circle coming on to Forrestal. Forrestal for once to my surprise became a yes-man and said he rather disagreed with me and believed that we ought to be more firm with the Russians and hold them up. I had pointed out that I believed in firmness on the minor matters where we had been yielding in the past . . . but I said that this was too big a question to take chances on; and so it went on. Harriman . . . was there and also General Deane of the American mission. They have been suffering personally from the Russians' behavior in minor matters for a long time and they have been urging firmness in dealing on these smaller matters and we have been backing them up; but now they were evidently influenced by their past bad treatment and they moved for strong words by the President on a strong position. And nobody backed me up until it came round to Marshall who wasn't called until towards the end. Then to my relief a brave man and a wise man spoke; and he said that he, like me, was troubled and urged caution.

You can see that the State Department has got itself into a mess. Contrary to what I thought was the wise course, they have not settled the problems that lie between the United States and Russia and Great Britain and France, the main powers, by wise negotiations before this public meeting in San Francisco, but they have gone ahead and called this great public meeting of all the United Nations, and they have got public opinion all churned up over it and now they feel compelled to bull the thing through. Why to me it seems that they might make trouble between us and Russia in comparison with which the whole possibilities of the San Francisco meeting amount to nothing. But it was a very embarrassing meeting and finally the President said good-bye to Forrestal and myself and Marshall . . . and said he was going to go on and talk the thing over and try to make up his mind with the others.

25   FROM   *Stalin to Truman:*
           "Poland Borders with Soviet Union,
         What Cannot be Said of Great Britain
            and the United States" (April 24, 1945)

After the strategy session on April 23, Truman told Molotov that the Polish govern-
ment would have to be reorganized. The President then sent a message to that effect to
Stalin. The following day, April 24, Stalin replied. He flatly refused to change the

SOURCE. U.S. Department of State, *Foreign Relations of the United States, Volume V,*
Europe (Washington, D.C.: 1967), pp. 263–264.

"kernel" of the Polish government. The conciliatory tone of his letter to Roosevelt on April 7 was missing. In what other respects does the note of the 24th differ from his earlier statements to Roosevelt and Churchill on the Polish issue?

MARSHAL STALIN TO PRESIDENT TRUMAN

I have received . . . on April 24 the message transmitted to me through V. M. Molotov.

1. From these messages it is clear that you continue to consider the Provisional Polish Government not as a kernel for the future government of national unity, but just like one of the groups equal to any other group of Poles.

Such an understanding of the position of the Polish Government and such an attitude towards it is very difficult to reconcile with the decisions of the Crimea Conference on Poland. At the Crimea Conference all three of us, including also President Roosevelt, proceeded from the fact that the Provisional Polish Government, as the one now operating in Poland and enjoying the confidence and support of the majority of the Polish people, should be the kernel, i.e. the main part of the new reorganized government of nation unity. You, evidently, do not agree to such an understanding of the matter. . . .

2. It is also necessary to take into account the fact that Poland borders with the Soviet Union, what cannot be said of Great Britain and the United States.

The question on Poland has the same meaning for the security of the Soviet Union as the question [of] Belgium and Greece for the security of Great Britain.

You, apparently, do not agree that the Soviet Union has a right to make efforts that there should exist in Poland a government friendly toward the Soviet Union, and that the Soviet government cannot agree to existence in Poland of a government hostile toward it. Besides everything else, this is demanded by the blood of the Soviet people abundantly shed on the field of Poland in the name of liberation of Poland. I do not know whether there has been established in Greece a really representative government, and whether the government in Belgium is really democratic. The Soviet Union was not consulted when these governments were being established there. The Soviet

Government did not lay claim to interference in these affairs as it understands the whole importance of Belgium and Greece for the security of Great Britain.

It is not clear why, while the question on Poland is discussed it is not wanted to take into consideration the interests of the Soviet Union from the point of view of its security.

3. Such conditions must be recognized unusual when two governments—those of the United States and Great Britain—beforehand settle with the Polish question in which the Soviet Union is first of all and most of all interested and put the government of the U.S.S.R. in an unbearable position trying to dictate to it their demands.

I have to state that such a situation cannot favor a harmonious solution of the question on Poland.

4. I am ready to fulfil your request and do everything possible to reach a harmonious solution, but you demand too much of me. In other words, you demand that I renounce the interests of security of the Soviet Union, but I cannot turn against my country. . . .

26 FROM *Hopkins-Stalin Discussions on Poland (May 26–June 6, 1945)*

After the exchange of notes on April 23 and 24, the Polish dispute worsened. Stalin arrested sixteen leaders of the Polish underground, many of whose members were now opposing the Warsaw government and Soviet control. Stalin dismissed Chruchill's concern over those arrested with the remark that discussions would not be worthwhile because London and Washington refused to recognize the legitimate Polish government. When the European war ended on May 8, the United States suddenly stopped lend-lease to Russia and Great Britain. There were various reasons for this termination, some of which were related to domestic politics instead of international affairs. The Soviets, however, interpreted the move as an attempt to exert economic pressure against them. Some Washington officials had indeed urged termination for precisely this reason. Truman later admitted that the abrupt halt of aid was a "mistake." Harry Hopkins' journey to Moscow in late May helped to break the log-jam. Stalin again agreed to widen the representation of the London Poles in the Warsaw government, and on June 21 the various Polish factions finally announced an agreement. On July 5,

SOURCE. U.S. Dept. of State, *Foreign Relations of the United States, The Conference of Berlin*, I (Washington, D.C.: 1960), pp. 26–59, excerpts.

the eve of the Potsdam conference, the United States finally, if reluctantly, recognized
a Polish government which, although enlarged, remained firmly in the control of pro-
Communist Warsaw leaders. In the context of these discussions, what is the meaning of
Stalin's statement that "the Soviet system was not exportable"?

Mr. Hopkins said that he wished to state this position [on Poland] as clearly and as forcibly as he knew how. He said the question of Poland per se was not so important as the fact that it had become a symbol of our ability to work out problems with the Soviet Union. He said that we had no special interests in Poland and no special desire to see any particular kind of government. That we would accept any government in Poland which was desired by the Polish people and was at the same time friendly to the Soviet Government. He said that the people and Government of the United States felt that this was a problem which should be worked out jointly between the United States, the Soviet Union and Great Britain and that we felt that the Polish people should be given the right to free elections to choose their own government and their own system and that Poland should genuinely be independent. The Government and people of the United States were disturbed because the preliminary steps towards the reestablishment of Poland appeared to have been taken unilaterally by the Soviet Union together with the present Warsaw Government and that in fact the United States was completely excluded. . . .

Marshal Stalin replied that he wished Mr. Hopkins would take into consideration the following factors: He said it may seem strange although it appeared to be recognized in United States circles and Churchill in his speeches also recognized it, that the Soviet Government should wish for a friendly Poland. In the course of twenty five years the Germans had twice invaded Russia via Poland. Neither the British nor American people had experienced such German invasions which were a horrible thing to endure and the results of which were not easily forgotten. He said these Germany invasions were not warfare but were like the incursions of the Huns. He said that Germany had been able to do this because Poland had been regarded as a part of the *cordon sanitaire* around the Soviet Union and that previous European policy had been that Polish Governments must be hostile to Russia. In these circumstances either Poland had been too weak to oppose Germany or had let the Germans come through. Thus Poland had served as a corridor for the German attacks on

Russia. He said Poland's weakness and hostility had been a great source of weakness to the Soviet Union and had permitted the Germans to do what they wished in the East and also in the West since the two were mixed together. It is therefore in Russia's vital interest that Poland should be both strong and friendly. He said there was no intention on the part of the Soviet Union to interfere in Poland's internal affairs, that Poland would live under the parliamentary system which is like Czechoslovakia, Belgium and Holland and that any talk of an intention to Sovietize Poland was stupid. He said even the Polish leaders, some of whom were communists, were against the Soviet system since the Polish people did not desire collective farms or other aspects of the Soviet system. In this the Polish leaders were right since the Soviet system was not exportable— it must develop from within on the basis of a set of conditions which were not present in Poland. . . . He said that whether the United States wished it or not it was a world power and would have to accept world-wide interests. . . . For this reason he fully recognized the right of the United States as a world power to participate in the Polish question and that the Soviet interest in Poland does not in any way exclude those of England and the United States. . . .

[Stalin said] that in regard to the specific freedoms mentioned by Mr. Hopkins, they could only be applied in full in peace time, and even then with certain limitations. He said for example the fascist party, whose intention it was to overthrow democratic governments, could not be permitted to enjoy to the full extent these freedoms. He said secondly there were the limitations imposed by war. All states when they were threatened by war [or] their frontiers were not secure had found it necessary to introduce certain restrictions. This had been done in England, France, the Soviet Union and elsewhere and perhaps to a lesser extent in the United States which was protected by wide oceans. It is for these reasons that only in time of peace could considerations be given to the full application of these freedoms. . . . With reference to freedom of speech certain restrictions had to be imposed for military security. . . .

Mr. Hopkins said he thoroughly understood the Marshal's opinions. He added that when he had left the Crimea Conference [that is, the Yalta Conference] President Roosevelt had thought the Polish matter was virtually settled. . . . Mr. Hopkins said that he must say that rightly or wrongly there was a strong feeling among the American people that the Soviet Union wished to dominate Poland. He added that was not his point of view but it was widely held in the United

States and that friends of international collaboration were wondering how it would be possible to work things out with the Soviet Union if we could not agree on the Polish question. . . .

CHAPTER V
GERMANY

27   FROM   *The Morgenthau Plan*
The Design for a De-Industrialized, Partitioned
Germany (September, 1944)

The division of Poland was the result, not a cause, of the Cold War. In historical perspective the German problem remains perhaps the most important of all such immediate postwar results. [*The Soviet Union and the United States fully understood that control of Germany was the key to the control of Europe.*] *That nation was the industrial power-house on the continent (twenty-five years after being annihilated in the war, Germany manufactured 40 percent of the total industrial goods produced by the six Common Market countries). Its ability to recover from a devastating conflict and to rebuild a military machine had been fully demonstrated in the 1919–1939 years. That was one reason, as Stalin stormed at Djilas, that the unity of the Slavs was important. Being the key to Europe, Germany, like Europe, was finally partitioned as the result of the U.S.–Soviet struggle.*

The first important American proposal dealing with postwar Germany was advanced by Secretary of the Treasury Henry Morgenthau, Jr., in September 1944. Later unfairly labeled as a "sell-out" to Communism, the Morgenthau Plan was quite sophisticated, particularly when combined with Morgenthau's suggestion that the United States provide Russia with a huge credit in return for particular economic concessions from the Soviets.] With these two policies, Morgenthau (1) suggested a way of removing the threat of a revived and militaristic Germany, the fear of which was a critical factor in Russian postwar plans; (2) proposed giving Russia sufficient economic aid so that Stalin would have less reason to block off and exploit Eastern Europe in order to reconstruct the Soviet economy; and (3) outlined a method whereby Soviet–American relations could be placed on an economic basis that would yield valuable benefits to the United States. Does the Morgenthau Plan for Germany fit within the broad policy of Luce's American Century, or is Morgenthau's proposal contrary to Luce's strategy?

SOURCE. The original document is reprinted in Henry Morgenthau, Jr., *Germany is Our Problem* (New York: 1945). Reprinted by permission of Harper & Row Publishers.

TOP SECRET: PROGRAM TO PREVENT FROM
STARTING A WORLD WAR III

1. Demilitarization of Germany. It should be the aim of the Allied Forces to accomplish the complete demilitarization of Germany in the shortest possible period of time after surrender. This means completely disarming the German Army and people (including the removal or destruction of all war material), the total destruction of the whole German armament industry, and the removal or destruction of other key industries which are basic to military strength.

2. New Boundaries of Germany.

(a) Poland should get that part of East Prussia which doesn't go to the U.S.S.R. and the southern portion of Silesia.

(b) France should get the Saar and the adjacent territories bounded by the Rhine and the Moselle Rivers.

(c) As indicated in 4 below an International Zone should be created containing the Ruhr and the surrounding industrial areas.

3. Partitioning of New Germany. The remaining portion of Germany should be divided into two autonomous, independent states, (a) a South German state comprising Bavaria, Wuerttemberg, Baden and some smaller areas and (b) a North German state comprising a large part of the old state of Prussia, Saxony, Thuringia and several smaller states.

There shall be a custom union between the new South German state and Austria, which will be restored to her pre-1938 political borders.

4. The Ruhr Area. (The Ruhr, surrounding industrial areas, including the Rhineland, the Keil Canal, and all German territory north of the Keil Canal.)

Here lies the heart of German industrial power. This area should not only be stripped of all presently existing industries; but so weakened and controlled that it can not in the foreseeable future become an industrial area. The following steps will accomplish this:

(a) Within a short period, if possible not longer than 6 months after the cessation of hostilities, all industrial plants and equipment not destroyed by military action shall be completely dismantled and transported to Allied Nations as restitution. All equipment be removed from the mines and the mines closed.

(b) The area should be made an international zone to be governed by an international security organization to be established by the United Nations. In governing the area the international organization should be guided by policies designed to further the above stated objective.

5. *Restitution and Reparation.* Reparations, in the form of future payments and deliveries, should not be demanded. Restitution and reparation shall be effected by the transfer of existing German resources and territories, e.g.,

(a) by restitution of property looted by the Germans in territories occupied by them;

(b) by transfer of German territory and German private rights in industrial property situated in such territory to invaded countries and the international organization under the program of partition;

(c) by the removal and distribution among devastated countries of industrial plants and equipment situated within the International Zone and the North and South German states delimited in the section on partition;

(d) by forced German labor outside Germany; and

(e) by confiscation of all German assets of any character whatsoever outside of Germany.

6. *Education and Propaganda.*

(a) All schools and universities will be closed until an Allied commission of Education has formulated an effective reorganization program. It is contemplated that it may require a considerable period of time before any institutions of higher education are reopened. Meanwhile the education of German students in foreign universities will not be prohibited. Elementary schools will be reopened as quickly as appropriate teachers and textbooks are available.

(b) All German radio stations and newspapers, magazines, weeklies, etc. shall be discontinued until adequate controls are established and an appropriate program formulated.

7. *Political Decentralization.* The military administration in Germany in the initial period should be carried out with a view toward the eventual partitioning of Germany. To facilitate partitioning and to assure its permanence the military authorities should be guided by the following principles:

(a) Dismiss all policy-making officials of the Reich government and deal primarily with local governents.

((b) Encourage the reestablishment of state governments in each of the states (Lander) corresponding to 18 states into which Germany is presently divided and in addition make the Prussian provinces separate states.

(c) Upon the partition of Germany, the various state governments should be encouraged to organize a federal government for each of the newly partitioned areas. Such new governments should be in the form of a confederation of states, with emphasis on states' rights and a large degree of local autonomy.

8. Responsibility of Military for Local German Economy. The sole purpose of the military in control of the German economy shall be to facilitate military operations and military occupation. The Allied Military Government shall not assume responsibility for such economic problems as price controls, rationing, unemployment, production, reconstruction, distribution, consumption, housing, or transportation, or take any measures designed to maintain or strengthen the German economy, except those which are essential to military operations. The responsibility for sustaining the German economy and people rests with the German people with such facilities as may be available under the circumstances.

9. Controls Over Development of German Economy. During a period of at least twenty years after surrender adequate controls, including controls over foreign trade and tight restrictions on capital imports, shall be maintained by the United Nations designed to prevent in the newly-established states the establishment or expansion of key industries basic to the German military potential and to control other key industries.

10. Agrarian Program. All large estates should be broken up and divided among the peasants and the system of primogeniture and entail should be abolished.

11. .Punishment of War Crimes and Treatment of Special Groups. A program for the punishment of certain war crimes and for the treatment of Nazi organizations and other special groups is contained in section 11 [not printed].

12. Uniforms and Parades.

(a) No German shall be permitted to wear, after an appropriate period of time following the cessation of hostilities, any military uniform or any uniform of any quasi military organizations.

(b) No military parades shall be permitted anywhere in Germany and all military bands shall be disbanded.

13. Aircraft. All aircraft (including gliders), whether military or commercial, will be confiscated for later disposition. No German shall be permitted to operate or to help operate any aircraft, including those owned by foreign interests.

14. United States Responsibilities.   Although the United States would have full military and civilian representation on whatever international commission or commissions may be established for the execution of the whole German program, the primary responsibility for the policing of Germany and for civil administration in Germany should be assumed by the military forces of Germany's continental neighbors. Specifically, these should include Russian, French, Polish, Czech, Yugoslav, Norwegian, Dutch and Belgian soldiers.

Under this program United States troops could be withdrawn within a relatively short time.

28 FROM   *Henry Morgenthau, Jr.*

The Meaning for Russia of the Morgenthau Plan on Germany (January 1945)

It seemed for a brief time in the autumn of 1944 that the Morgenthau Plan would be adopted by President Roosevelt as the American strategy for reconstructing Germany after the war. By early winter, however, Roosevelt was changing his mind. Secretary of War Henry Stimson, Secretary of State Cordell Hull, and American Ambassador to Russia W. Averell Harriman were vigorously objecting to the proposal. As the President prepared to leave for the Yalta Conference, Morgenthau, as the following selections reveal, made an earnest effort to convince Roosevelt that the Secretary's original plan should be followed. Do the two memoranda indicate that, as later critics charged, the Morgenthau Plan was "soft" on Communism in Central Europe?

UNSENT MEMORANDUM, PREPARED BY MORGENTHAU FOR ROOSEVELT, JANUARY 10, 1945

The more I think of this problem, and the more I read and hear discussions of it, the clearer it seems to me that the real motive of most of those who oppose a weak Germany is not any actual disagreement on these three points [that is, that the Germans would continue

SOURCE. The first selection is from John Morton Blum, *From the Morgenthau Diaries, Years of War, 1941–1945* (Boston: 1967), pp. 394–395. Reprinted by permission of Houghton Mifflin Company. The second selection is from U.S. Dept. of State, *Foreign Relations of the United States, 1945, Volume V, Europe* (Washington, D.C: 1967), pp. 948–949.

to have the will to conquer the world again, that mere reeducation and democracy could not remove that will, and that it was heavy industry which made Germany militarily dangerous]. [On the contrary, it is simply an expression of fear of Russia and communism.] It is the twenty-year-old idea of a "bulwark against Bolshevism"—which was one of the factors which brought this present war down on us. Because the people who hold this view are unwilling (for reasons which, no doubt, they regard as statesmanlike) to come out in the open and lay the real issue on the table, all sorts of smoke screens are thrown up to support the proposition that Germany must be rebuilt. Examples are:

1. The fallacy that Europe needs a strong industrial Germany.

2. The contention that recurring reparations (which would require immediate reconstruction of the German economy) are necessary so that Germany may be made to pay for the destruction she has caused.

3. The naive belief that the removal or destruction of all German war materials and the German armament industry would in itself prevent Germany from waging another war.

4. The illogal assumption that a soft peace would facilitate the growth of democracy in Germany.

5. The fallacy that making Germany a predominately agricultural country, with light industries but no heavy industries, would mean starving Germans . . .

This thing needs to be dragged out into the open. I feel so deeply about it that I speak strongly. If we don't face it I am just as sure as I can be that we are going to let a lot of hollow and hypocritical propaganda lead us into recreating a strong Germany and making a foe of Russia. I shudder for the sake of our children to think of what will follow.

There is nothing that I can think of that can do more at this moment to engender trust or distrust between the United States and Russia than the position this Government takes on the German problem.

MEMORANDUM FROM MORGENTHAU TO ROOSEVELT,
JANUARY 10, 1945

I suggest consideration be given to a financial arrangement with the U.S.S.R. to provide her with $10 billion credits for the purchase of reconstruction goods in the U.S., with provision for repayment to us chiefly in strategic raw materials in short supply in the U.S.

1. The interest rate could be 2%, amortized over a period of 35 years. . . .

2. The Russians have more than adequate means to assure full repayment. There are three principal sources from which she can obtain the necessary amount of dollars.

(a) Selling to us strategic raw materials which are in short supply in the U.S. because of our depleted natural resources.

(b) Russia will be able to develop substantial dollar assets from tourist trade, exports of non-strategic items to the U.S., and from a favorable balance of trade with the rest of the world.

(c) Russia has a stock of gold estimated at $2 billion now and is reported to be able to produce from $150 to $250 million per year. These gold resources can be used to pay her obligations to the United States to the extent that her other dollar sources are not adequate.

3. An important feature of this proposal is that we will be conserving our depleted natural resources by drawing on Russia's huge reserves for current needs of industrial raw materials in short supply here. We would be able to obtain a provision in the financial agreement whereby we could call upon Russia for whatever raw materials we need without giving a commitment on our part to buy.

4. This credit to Russia would be a major step in your program to provide 60 million jobs in the post-war period.

29   FROM   *W. Averell Harriman*

Aid for Russian Reconstruction Should Depend Upon Soviet Behavior in International Matters (January 4 and 6, 1945).

By the eve of the Yalta conference, the American Ambassador to Russia W. Averell Harriman was a leading opponent of Morgenthau's proposals. Harriman particularly objected to Morgenthau's belief that the controlled reconstruction of Germany should be accompanied by massive economic aid for the Soviets. The issue came to the forefront on January 4, 1945 when Foreign Minister V. M. Molotov formally asked Harriman for long-term American credit to the Soviet Union. The Ambassador's views, sent to

SOURCE. U.S. Dept, of State, *Foreign Relations of the United States, 1945, Volume V, Europe* (Washington, D.C.: 1967), pp. 942–947.

Washington in a telegram of January 6, became standard American policy. No extensive discussions about a loan or credits were held with the Soviets. Morgenthau was particularly bitter that the issue was not raised by Roosevelt at Yalta during his discussions with Stalin. On which points do Harriman and Morgenthau agree in their general assessment of the Soviet Union?

AMBASSADOR IN THE SOVIET UNION (HARRIMAN) TO THE SECRETARY OF STATE, JANUARY 4, 1945

At Molotov's invitation, I called on him last night. He handed me an *aide-mémoire* dated January 3 the substance of which was as follows:

"[On October 31st] it was stated that the Soviet Government would put forward for our Government's consideration its proposals for a long-term credit to the Soviet Union. The Soviet Government accordingly wishes to state the following: Having a mind the repeated statements of American public figures concerning the desirability of receiving extensive large Soviet orders for the postwar and transition period, the Soviet Government considers it possible to place orders on the basis of long-term credits to the amount of 6 billion dollars. . . . The credits should run for 30 years, amortization to begin on the last day of the 9th year and to end on the last day of the 30th year. . . ."

AMBASSADOR IN THE SOVIET UNION (HARRIMAN) TO THE SECRETARY OF STATE, JANUARY 6, 1945

Now that I have recovered from my surprise at Molotov's strange procedure in initiating discussions regarding a post-war credit in such a detailed *aide-mémoire*, I believe the Department will be interested in receiving my reactions.

1. I feel we should entirely disregard the unconventional character of the document and the unreasonableness of its terms and chalk it up to ignorance of normal business procedures and the strange ideas of the Russians on how to get the best trade. From our experience it has become increasingly my impression that Mikoyan [Anastas Mikoyan, People's Commissar for Foreign Trade of the Soviet Union] has not divorced himself from his Armenian background. He starts negotiations on the basis of "twice as much for half the price" and then gives in bit by bit expecting in the process to wear us out.

2. Molotov made it very plain that the Soviet Government placed

high importance on a large postwar credit as a basis for the development of "Soviet-American relations". From his statement I sensed an implication that the development of our friendly relations would depend upon a generous credit. [It is of course my very strong and earnest opinion that the question of the credit should be tied into our overall diplomatic relations with the Soviet Union and at the appropriate time the Russians should be given to understand that our willingness to cooperate wholeheartedly with them in their vast reconstruction problems will depend upon their behavior in international matters. I feel, too, that the eventual Lend-Lease settlement should also be borne in mind in this connection.

3. It would seem probable that the timing of the delivery of this note had in mind the prospects of "a meeting" [that is, the Big Three meeting to be held in February at Yalta]. I interpret it therefore to indicate that should there be a meeting the Russians would expect this subject to be discussed.

4. It would seem that the time had arrived when our Government's policy should be crystallized and a decision reached on what we are prepared to do provided other aspects of our relations develop satisfactorily.

5. It is my basic conviction that we should do everything we can to assist the Soviet Union through credits in developing a sound economy. I feel strongly that the sooner the Soviet Union can develop a decent life for its people the more tolerant they will become. One has to live in Russia a considerable period of time to appreciate fully the unbelievably low standards which prevail among the Russian people and the extent to which this affects their outlook. The Soviet Government has proved in this war that it can organize production effectively and I am satisfied that the great urge of Stalin and his associates is to provide a better physical life for the Russian people, although they will retain a substantial military establishment.

6. I believe that the United States Government should retain control of any credits granted in order that the political advantages may be retained and that we may be satisfied the equipment purchased is for purposes that meet our general approval. . . .

30   FROM   *U.S. Department of State*
     A Partitioned Germany Will Keep the World in Lasting
                Perturbation (June 29, 1945)

After Ambassador Harriman and others successfully blocked Morgenthau's pro-
posal for extending credits to the Soviets, the State Department and Secretary of War
Henry Stimson fought other parts of the Morgenthau Plan. They convinced Presidents
Roosevelt and Truman that in order to prevent the development of exclusive spheres,
and if all of Europe was to be restored economically, Germany must be kept whole and
industrialized. This policy was laid out in detail in a Briefing Book Paper on Germany,
prepared by State Department experts for President Truman's use at the Potsdam
Conference. Is the conclusion of the following Briefing Paper essentially that it is
impossible to keep Germany under control?

RECOMMENDATION

It is recommended that this Government oppose the partition of
Germany into two or more separate states as distinct from border
cessions or readjustments.

DISCUSSION

Previous Considerations.   When the question of a possible dismemberment of Germany as a security measure was first discussed in governmental circles in Washington, the late President Roosevelt was disposed
to favor the proposal. At the Tehran Conference it is understood that
he was prepared to see Germany divided into five separate states. By
the time of the Crimea Conference, [Yalta], however, he had recon-
sidered his original judgment and expressed himself in opposition
to considering partition prior to termination of hostilities and an
opportunity to study actual conditions and trends in Germany. He
agreed, none the less, to a modification of the original instrument
of unconditional surrender to provide for German recognition of the
right of the victor powers to dismember Germany if they deemed it
desirable. It was further agreed that a committee consisting of Ambas-

SOURCE. U.S. Dept. of State, *Foreign Relations of the United States, The Conference of*
Berlin, I (Washington, D.C.: 1960), pp. 456–461.

sador Winant [for the U.S.], Ambassador Gousev [for the Soviet Union], and Mr. Eden [for the British] should study the procedure for effecting dismemberment and whether it appeared desirable.

The committee at its first meeting in London decided to consider not only procedures but also the prior questions of the desirability and the feasibility of dismemberment. In comment on the report of this meeting, Mr. Roosevelt wrote on April 6, "I think our attitude should be one of study and postponement of final decision." The committee has not had further meetings.

In the Department of State the Committee on Post-War Programs, composed of the higher officers of the Department, in May 1944 unanimously approved a recommendation of the Inter-Divisional Committee on Germany that this Government oppose the forcible partition of Germany.

The Bases of the Recommendation. Opposition to partition rests on the following considerations:

Partition as a device for stripping the Germans of the ability to make war would necessitate a genuine and lasting dispersal of their national energies. This dispersal would imply prevention of political and military collaboration and, to be effective, would likewise entail a break-up of Germany's economic unity since, without it, a political dismemberment would be useless.

It is submitted that such a program is unnecessary as a security measure, that it would be injurious to the economic rehabilitation of Europe, and that it would be a source of disturbance and danger to the peace of Europe rather than a source of tranquillity.

Partition could not for some time to come be trusted as a substitute for the basic demilitarization controls which, if adequately enforced, would provide adequate security. In the uncertainties of the coming years it would not be prudent to give up the strictest supervision of Germany's war-making potentialities whether Germany is divided or not. . . .

The best calculation is that the German people will not willingly accept dismemberment as a permanent fate. The growth of the sense of German national unity has been such that no significant group has questioned the verdict of 1871. . . .

It must be anticipated, consequently, that when the Germans have recovered somewhat from the shock of defeat their patriotic sense of national unity will again assert itself—unless the victors can discover and exploit some geographic lines of fissure within Germany. There seems at present little likelihood that such lines can be found.

The historic divisions of Germany offer little basis of hope. The old *Laender* provide at best some grounds for moderate decentralization. Religious differences . . . indicate no substantial cleavage. The historic differences between East and West on the one hand and North and South on the other have virtually no substance in contemporary Germany. . . .

These considerations indicate, accordingly, that the four zones of military occupation would offer no prospect of serving as effective lines of internal cleavage and therefore of partition, and they were certainly not drawn for the purpose of partition.

The only tenable calculation is that partition, regardless of the number of partite states and their specific boundaries, would have to be maintained indefinitely by force. . . .

It should furthermore be emphasized that a partition of Germany could also result in a highly dangerous competition on the part of various states to control or to influence the governments of the partite states. The Germans will thereby be enabled to play off one ally against another in pursuance of what could well form a common plan on their part. By inviting the east or the west to stake out special claims and exert a predominant role in one or more of the new states, the Germans might well obtain special concessions for one state or another and jeopardize the unity of the Allies in preventing the renewal of German aggression. The skill with which the Germans played one power off against another during the Hitler period is evidence of their capacity to take every advantage of the political possibilities that would be provided by the establishment of several German States. . . .

The result of such a state of affairs might be a Germany unable to make war but nonetheless a Germany able to keep the world in lasting perturbation. . . .

Since at the present, when most of the world is embittered by Nazi misdeeds, almost no responsible statesman and few voices of public opinion in Europe favor partition, it would be prudent to anticipate the time when partition, if imposed, would appear unjust and economically bad and one or more of the enforcing powers would refuse further responsibility for it.

That possibility, with its disastrous consequences for the whole program of control, might well counsel the adoption of a program of restraint that would not lend itself to a reversal of policy when the dangers of Germany's aggressive militarism are not so poignantly felt as during and immediately after the war.

31   FROM   *Secretary of War Henry Stimson:*
German Industry Must be Restored (July 16, 1945)

On the eve of the Postsdam Conference in July, 1945, Morgenthau made one last attempt to convince Truman that a different approach must be made to Russia on the German question. The President responded by accepting Morgenthau's resignation as Secretary of the Treasury. Stimson, not Morgenthau, accompanied Truman to Potsdam. At the beginning of the conference, the Secretary of War explained in a "Memorandum for the President" why a revived Germany was essential for a revived, healthy, non-Communist Europe. How might Morgenthau have critized Stimson's memorandum?

MEMORANDUM FOR THE PRESIDENT

We have occupied Germany following a devastating conquest which has laid waste wide areas of middle Europe, extending from France to well within the boundaries of Russia, and extending from the North Sea and the Baltic to the Mediterranean. Germany, which has been responsible for loosing the forces which resulted in the two World Wars, is herself laid waste and is in the geographical center of the area of devastation. . . .

On the one hand it is clear that Germany has created, and twice misused, a swollen war industry—one substantially beyond her peaceful needs, and even though this capacity has been greatly impaired by defeat, certain physical steps can and should be taken to hamper the regrowth of her industrial capacity to more than reasonable peacetime needs.

On the other hand from the point of view of general European recovery it seems even more important that the area again be made useful and productive. [Considering Germany alone, the figures show that the commerce of Europe was very largely predicated upon her industry.] There was a period, substantially before the war, when Germany became the largest source of supply to ten European countries—viz. Russia, Norway, Sweden, Denmark, Holland, Switzerland, Italy, Austria-Hungary, Roumania and Bulgaria, and the second largest supplier of Great Britain, Belgium and France. At the same time she became the best customer of Russia, Norway, Holland,

[handwritten margin notes: Germany key to Europe economic revival]

SOURCE. U.S. Dept. of State, *Foreign Relations of the United States, The Conference of Berlin*, II (Washington, D.C.: 1960), pp. 754–757.

Belgium, Switzerland, Italy, and Austria-Hungary, and the second best of Great Britain, Sweden and Denmark. . . .

It is my view that it would be foolish, dangerous and provocative of future wars to adopt a program calling for the major destruction of Germany's industry and resources. Not only would any reasonable prospect for the reestablishment of European industry be dissipated by such action, but such destruction would be bound to leave a focus of economic and political infection which might well destroy all hope we have of encouraging democratic thinking and practices in Europe. What elements of German industry can be destroyed or removed as unnecessary for peacetime needs is a matter of [for?] expert determination. The balance must be put to work as soon as practicable and subjected to some system of security control. It is a task requiring perseverance, application and intelligence over a long period of time, but I am certain that mere destruction is neither effective as a security measure, nor, in the light of European, including German needs, possible as an economic one.

The need of all Europe includes the prompt stimulation of production within Germany, of food, coal, clothing, and housing. Production of these items is not capable of independent development. It must be based on other items and services, in short, general industry and trade. Without freedom of internal trade and communication, no one of these items can be produced on the scale which will be required. It follows that we cannot afford to operate Germany as if she were four separate water tight compartments.

Accordingly, as a first step, I would urge the adoption by the Great Powers at the Conference [at Potsdam] of a policy which would treat Germany as an economic unit so as to permit her to contribute to her own and to general European rehabilitation. . . .

32 FROM *Churchill, Stalin, and Truman:*
A Bitter Discussion Over the Dismemberment
of Germany (July 21, 1945)

The German policy of the Harriman-Stimson group did not assure the Russians that Germany would not again become aggressive. Stalin was particularly concerned with two aspects of the German problem. First, he was determined that Germany not

SOURCE. U.S. Dept. of State, *Foreign Relations of the United States, The Conference of Berlin*, **II**, (Washington, D.C.: 1960), pp. 217–221.

be allowed to pose another military threat to the Soviet Union. He partially accomplished that objective by giving a portion of Eastern Germany to Poland (in compensation for the territory which Russia absorbed from the Poles), despite the bitter objections of Truman and Churchill at the Potsdam Conference. Second, he believed that the Soviets had a right to claim large amounts of German industrial machinery, manufactures, and agricultural produce as reparation for the German devastation of Russia. These reparations, moreover, became imperative if the Soviets hoped to rebuild their own economy rapidly. This second objective worked at cross-purposes with the Stimson policy for Germany, since the Germans could not help to rebuild a viable Europe if their machinery and products were moving in large amounts to Russia. The climactic discussion at Postdam on these issues came on July 21. Who is dealing from strength in this debate?

FIFTH PLENARY MEETING AT THE POTSDAM CONFERENCE, JULY 21, 1945

Truman: I propose that the matters of the Polish frontier be considered at the peace conference [after the war is concluded] after consultation with the Polish government of national unity. We decided that Germany with 1937 boundaries should be considered [the] starting point. We decided on our zones. We moved our troops to the zones assigned to us. Now another occupying government [Poland] has been assigned a zone without consultation with us. We can not arrive at reparations and other problems of Germany if Germany is divided up before the peace conference. I am very friendly to Poland and sympathetic with what Russia proposes regarding the western frontier, but I do not want to do it that way.

Stalin: The Crimea [Yalta] decision was that the eastern frontier of Poland should follow the Curzon line. As to the western frontier, it was decided that Poland was to receive territory in the west and north in compensation.

Truman: That is right, but I am against assigning an occupation zone to Poland. . . .

Stalin: Our view is that we should express our view in accordance with that of the Polish government, but final question should be left to the peace conference. As to our giving the Poles a zone of occupation without consulting the other powers, this is not accurate. We received several proposals from the American and British governments that we should not permit the Poles in the disputed western frontier area. We could not follow this because German population fled and Poles remained. Our armies needed local administrations. Our armies are not set up to fight and clear country of enemy agents at the same time. We so informed our British and American friends. The more ready we were to let the Polish administration function, the more we were sure the Poles would receive territory to the west. I do not see the harm of permitting the Poles to set up administrations in territories in which they are to remain.

Truman: I wanted the administrations in the four zones to be as we have agreed. We can not agree on reparations if parts of Germany are given away.

Stalin: We are concerned about reparations but we will take this risk. . . .

Churchill: It is from these regions that a very important part of the supplies from which Germany is to be fed come.

Stalin: Who will work in these areas? There is no one but the Poles who will plow the land.

Truman: The question is not who occupies the country, but how we stand on the question as to who is to occupy Germany. I want it understood that the Soviet [Union] is occupying this zone and is responsible for it. I don't think we are far apart on our conclusions.

Stalin: On paper it is formerly German territory but in fact it is Polish territory. There are no Germans left. The Soviet [Union] is responsible for the territory.

Truman: Where are the nine million Germans?

Stalin: They have fled.

Churchill: How can they be fed? I am told that under the Polish plan put forward by the Soviets that a quarter of arable land of Germany would be alienated—one-fourth of all the arable land from which German food and reparations must come. The Poles come from the East but 8¼ [8½?] million Germans are [displaced]. It is apparent that a disproportionate part of the population will be cast on the rest of Germany with its food supplies alienated.

Truman: France wants the Saar and the Ruhr. What will be left?

Stalin: As regards the claims of France, we have made no decision. As to the Poles, we have. . . .

Churchill: Of course I am deeply committed to compensate Poland for what has been taken from her, but I thought there should be a balance. Poland is now claiming a [sic] vastly more territory than she gave up. I can not concede that such an extravagant movement of populations should occur. So vast a movement of population will be a great shock to public opinion to [in] my country at least. It puts us in a position that I can not possibly defend. I do not think it is good for Poland. If the Germans have run out they should be encouraged to return. The Poles have no right to create a catastrophe in the feeding of Germany. . . . If enough food is not found we may be confronted with conditions like those in the German concentration camps, even on a vaster scale.

Stalin: Germany has never done without the import of grain. Let Germany buy more bread from Poland. The territory is cultivated by the Poles, not the Germans.

Churchill: In addition, the condition of this territory into which Poles are being introduced is most peculiar. I am told the Poles are selling coal from Silesia to Sweden when we in England must go through a bitter, fireless winter, worse than that experienced during the war. We stand on the general principle that the supply of food of 1937 Germany should be available for the support of the German people irrespective of the zones of occupation.

Stalin: But who is to produce the coal? It is the Poles who are mining the coal.

Churchill: They fled from the cannons. Now that the firing has ceased they should come back.

Stalin: We have little sympathy with these scoundrels and war criminals.

Churchill: I was impressed by what the Marshal [Stalin] said yesterday about not letting past bitterness color our decisions.

Stalin: What I said yesterday does not apply to war criminals. I had in mind only the proprietors who have fled. We ourselves are purchasing coal from the Poles who are mining it.

Truman: I am concerned that a piece of Germany, a valuable piece has been cut off. This must be deemed a part of Germany in considering reparations and in the feeding of Germany. The Poles have no right to seize this territory now and take it out of the peace settlement. Are we going to maintain occupied zones until the peace or are we going to give Germany away piece-meal?

Stalin: Nobody can exploit this region but the Poles. . . .

Churchill: This situation creates difficulties for us as well as for the Germans.

Stalin: We may have to create further difficulty for the Germans then. The less industry we leave in Germany, the more markets there will be for your goods. We have destroyed for you a competitor with low living standards and low prices. . . .

Truman: I shall state frankly what I think. I can not consent to the removal of eastern Germany from contributing to the economy of the whole of Germany.

Stalin: Are we through?

Churchill: Can't we sleep on it?

Adjourned.

33 FROM *The Potsdam Agreement on Germany (August 1, 1945)*

Germany was the central issue at Potsdam, and the final agreement was reached only after long, angry debates. "The German people under a democracy would have been a far superior ally than Russia," Secretary of State James F. Byrnes told his staff privately. "There is too much difference in the ideologies of the U.S. and Russia to work out a long term program." Part of the American problem was Russia, but another difficulty was contradictions within the U.S. position. The President, for example, could not have both a "whole" Germany and a Germany which would be rapidly reconstructed economically, for if the nation was governed by the Four Powers as a whole, Russia would extract reparations from the entire area. The State Department doubted, moreover, that the Soviets would even allow Western observation of their zone in East Germany. The United States had to choose: it could have either a united Germany under Four-Power control, or a large portion of Germany safe from Soviet reparation demands, a portion which would serve as the seed for an economically revived Europe and a buffer zone separating the Communists from Western Europe. The United States chose the latter. At Potsdam, despite wording in the final agreement that Germany "shall be treated as a single economic unit," the nation was in fact divided. The final reparation settlement illustrated the division. Whereas at Yalta the Big Three had agreed to a total reparation sum of $20 billion to be extracted from a united Germany (with half going to the Soviet Union), the final settlement at Potsdam mentioned no specific figures. Instead, it gave percentages and recognized explicitly the strength of the Soviets and the Western powers in their respective occupation zones of Germany. Poland's occupation of Eastern Germany (the territory east of a line formed by the Oder and Neisse Rivers) was also recognized, although it was to be only "temporary." (Twenty-five years later, the Poles gave no signs of withdrawing from this "temporary" occupation.) In these ways, the three key German issues—dismemberment, reparations, and the Polish-German boundary—were decided at Potsdam. What is the actual effect of restoring "local responsibility" in an area such as the Germany of 1945?

SOURCE. U.S. Dept. of State, *Foreign Relations of the United States, The Conference of Berlin*, **II**, (Washington, D.C.: 1960), pp. 1481–1487.

POLITICAL PRINCIPLES

1. In accordance with the agreement on Control Machinery in Germany, supreme authority in Germany is exercised, on instructions from their respective Governments, by the Commander in Chief of the Armed Forces of the United States of America, the United Kingdom, the Union of Soviet Socialist Republics, and the French Republic, each in his own zone of occupation, and also jointly, in matters affecting Germany as a whole, in their capacity as members of the Control Council.

2. So far as is practicable, there shall be uniformity of treatment of the German population throughout Germany.

3. The purposes of the occupation of Germany by which the Control Council shall be guided are:

The complete disarmament and demilitarization of Germany and the elimination or control of all German industry that could be used for military production. To these ends:

All German land, naval and air forces, the S.S., S.A., S.D., and Gestapo, with all their organizations, staffs and institutions, including the general staff, the officers' corps, reserve corps, military schools, war veterans' organizations and all other military and quasi-military organizations, together with all clubs and associations which serve to keep alive the military tradition in Germany, shall be completely and finally abolished in such manner as permanently to prevent the revival or reorganization of German militarism and nazism.

[margin handwriting: Military abolished]

All arms, ammunition and implements of war and all specialized facilities for their production shall be held at the disposal of the Allies or destroyed. The maintenance and production of all aircraft and all arms, ammunition and implements of war shall be prevented.

To convince the German people that they have suffered a total military defeat and that they cannot escape responsibility for what they have brought upon themselves, since their own ruthless warfare and the fanatical Nazi resistance have destroyed German economy and made chaos and suffering inevitable.

[margin handwriting: Morganthau Plan redone]

To destroy the National Socialist Party and its affiliated and supervised organizations, to dissolve all Nazi institutions, to insure that they are not revived in any form, and to prevent all Nazi and militarist activity or propaganda. . . .

4. All Nazi laws which provided the basis of the Hitler regime or established discrimination on grounds of race, creed, or political

opinions shall be abolished. No such discriminations, whether legal, administrative or otherwise, shall be tolerated.

5. War criminals and those who have participated in planning or carrying out Nazi enterprises involving or resulting in atrocities or war crimes shall be arrested and brought to judgment. . . .

7. German education shall be so controlled as completely to eliminate Nazi and militarist doctrines and to make possible the successful development of democratic ideas.

8. The judicial system will be reorganized in accordance with the principles of democracy, of justice under law, and of equal rights for all citizens without distinction of race, nationality or religion.

9. The administration of affairs in Germany should be directed toward the decentralization of the political structure and the development of local responsibility. . . .

For the time being no central German Government shall be established. Notwithstanding this, however, certain essential central German administrative departments, headed by state secretaries, shall be established, particularly in the fields of finance, transport, communications, foreign trade and industry. Such departments will act under the direction of the Control Council.

10. Subject to the necessity for maintaining military security, freedom of speech, press and religion shall be permitted, and religious institutions shall be respected. Subject likewise to the maintenance of military security, the formation of free trade unions shall be permitted.

ECONOMIC PRINCIPLES

11. In order to eliminate Germany's war potential, the production of arms, ammunition and implements of war as well as all types of aircraft and sea-going ships, shall be prohibited and prevented. Production of metals, chemicals, machinery and other items that are directly necessary to a war economy shall be rigidly controlled and restricted to Germany's approved post-war peacetime needs to meet the objectives stated in Paragraph 15. Productive capacity not needed for permitted production shall be removed in accordance with the reparations plan recommended by the Allied Commission on reparations and approved by the Governments concerned, or if not removed shall be destroyed.

12. At the earliest practicable date the German economy shall

be decentralized for the purpose of eliminating the present excessive concentration of economic power as exemplified in particular by cartels, syndicates, trusts and other monopolistic arrangements.

13. In organizing the German economy, primary emphasis shall *Nrg.* be given to the development of agriculture and peaceful domestic *again* industries.

[14. During the period of occupation Germany shall be treated as a single economic unit.] . .   *Key to reparations*

15. Allied controls shall be imposed upon the German economy, but only to the extent necessary:

To carry out programs of industrial disarmament and demilitarization, of reparations, and of approved exports and imports.

To assure the production and maintenance of goods and services required to meet the needs of the occupying forces and displaced persons in Germany, and essential to maintain in Germany average living standards not exceeding the average of the standards of living of European countries. (European countries means all European countries, excluding the United Kingdom and the Union of Soviet Socialist Republics.). . . .

16. In the imposition and maintenance of economic controls established by the Control Council German administrative machinery shall be created and the German authorities shall be required to the fullest extent practicable to proclaim and assume administration of such controls. Thus it should be brought home to the German people that the responsibility for the administration of such controls and any breakdown in these controls will rest with themselves. Any German controls which may run counter to the objectives of occupation will be prohibited. . . .

REPARATIONS FROM GERMANY

In accordance with the Crimea decision that Germany be compelled to compensate to the greatest possible extent for the loss and suffering that she has caused to the United Nations and for which the German people cannot escape responsibility, the following agreement on reparations was reached:

1. Reparation claims of the U.S.S.R. shall be met by removals from the zone of Germany occupied by the U.S.S.R. and from appropriate German external assets.

Reparations to USSR

2. The U.S.S.R. undertakes to settle the reparation claims of Poland from its own share of reparations.

3. The reparation claims of the United States, the United Kingdom and other countries entitled to reparations shall be met from the western zones and from appropriate German external assets.

4. In addition to the reparations to be taken by the U.S.S.R. from its own zone of occupation, the U.S.S.R. shall receive additionally from the western zones:

Fifteen per cent of such usable and complete industrial capital equipment, in the first place from the metalurgical, chemical and machine manufacturing industries, as is unnecessary for the German peace economy and should be removed from the western zones of Germany, in exchange for an equivalent value of food, coal, potash, zinc, timber, clay products, petroleum products, and such other commodities as may be agreed upon.

Ten per cent of such industrial capital equipment as is unnecessary for the German peace economy and should be removed from the western zones, to be transferred to the Soviet Government on reparations account without payment or exchange of any kind in return.

Removals of equipment as provided in (a) and (b) above shall be made simultaneously.

5. The amount of equipment to be removed from the western zones on account of reparations must be determined within six months from now at the latest.

6. Removals of industrial capital equipment shall begin as soon as possible and shall be completed within two years from the determination specified in Paragraph 5. The delivery of products covered by 4 (a) above shall begin as soon as possible and shall be made by the U.S.S.R. in agreed installments within five years of the date hereof. The determination of the amount and character of the industrial capital equipment unnecessary for the German peace economy and therefore available for reparations shall be made by the Control Council under policies fixed by the Allied Commission on Reparations, with the participation of France, subject to the final approval of the zone commander in the zone from which the equipment is to be removed. . . .

7. The Soviet Government renounces all claims in respect of reparations to shares of German enterprises which are located in the western zones of occupation in Germany, as well as to German foreign assets in all countries, except those specified in Paragraph 9 below.

8. The Governments of the United Kingdom and the United States of America renounce their claims in respect of reparations to shares of German enterprises which are located in the eastern zone of occupation in Germany, as well as to German foreign assets in Bulgaria, Finland, Hungary, Rumania and eastern Austria.

9. The Soviet Government makes no claims to gold captured by the Allied troops in Germany.

34   FROM   *Alfred P. Sloan*
General Motors Prefers an Industrialized Germany
(November 30, 1945)

The desire on the part of the State Department and Stimson to keep Germany industrialized and economically viable was motivated not solely by concerns about Soviet or European policy. A reconstructed Germany and a prosperous Western Europe was essential for the American economy. Leading American businessmen, confronted with the need to make the rapid and dangerous transition from a war to peace economy, fully appreciated the place of Germany in the postwar economic picture. In the following selection, Alfred P. Sloan, Chairman of the Board of General Motors, explains to Bernard Baruch that Germany must be industrialized. Sloan even argues that the Potsdam agreement too closely resembles the Morgenthau Plan, Baruch had taken the position that only strong controls could prevent a resurgence of German nationalism and aggression. Note Sloan's disdain of France and the Morgenthau Plan. He does not mention the Soviet Union, but what are the implications of his letter for Russian–American relations?

My dear Mr. Baruch: Thanks ever so much for your kind letter of November 19th. . . . Pre-war General Motors Corporation had, as you know, very important interests in Germany.

My personal conviction is—and I think this will be self-evident before very long—that the economic policy laid down by the Potsdam agreement, as to Germany, will be recognized and accepted as a complete failure. It was bound to be from its inception. It is in-

SOURCE. Alfred P. Sloan, Chairman of the Board of General Motors Corporation, to Bernard M. Baruch, November 30, 1945, Bernard M. Baruch papers, Princeton University Library. Reprinted by permission.

evitable that if such a line of procedure is followed and Germany
is reduced to an agricultural state, then we in the United States will
have to be taxed to feed and maintain them. And that will not go very
far from the standpoint of the American thinking. It will simply
accelerate the trend toward isolationism. . . .

Now I recognize that if the production facilities formerly in
Germany were eliminated it is bound to stimulate, in degree, the
business opportunities of adjacent countries including England
and incidentally ourselves. But I want to point out to you—and I
say this from intimate experience in a broad way—the other countries
that you mention are just not comparable with Germany in their
efficiency, their ability to produce, their willingness to work, and
all the other things that form the foundation stones of an industrial
development and production on the basis of efficiency. So far as we
in General Motors are concerned, we were glad to have been able to
operate in Germany, prewar, and it was frequently passed on to us
by the German Economic Ministry that we had contributed much to
the expansion of industry in Germany and to the advancement of their
technological position in the areas in which we were operating.

But, on the other hand, when it comes to operating in some of the
countries that you mention on the second page of your letter, we
would not be at all interested. For instance: There is nothing that
could convince us in General Motors that it was either sound or
desirable or worth while to undertake an operation of any con-
sequence in a country like France.

. . . I repeat: You can't take approximately sixty-five million
people; industrious people, intelligent, willing to work and having
almost all the characteristics that leads to business success and reduce
them to a state of slavery without the whole world losing much and
gaining nothing. I am thoroughly convinced that it will come out
that way.

I accept what you say about production being of no avail to
humanity that is being used for military world power. There is no
question about that. That is an important part of the problem. As to
that particular point, I still believe that if we are prepared to carry
through into the years to come and prevent Germany from beginning
to do the things that we now say they can't do and meet the issue when
the issue arises, as it surely will, then we can just as well exercise
control over what they do in a military way.

I want to point out to you again most emphatically, that one thing
is not appreciated in this whole argument and that is: the various

processes of production involving technological progress, facilities, materials and all the other things necessary for a modern economy are so closely interwoven with the possibilities of war that you just can't make any separation. You have either got to go one way or the other. If we decide that everything shall be eliminated that leads to war, directly or indirectly, then we must accept the Morgenthau philosophy. If we take the position suggested in the second paragraph of your letter, then the Morgenthau philosophy is o-u-t and we must necessarily exercise control in relation to production for certain specific things applicable to war purposes. . . .

35 FROM *Secretary of State James F. Byrnes* *The Stuttgart Speech (September 6, 1946)*

Economic relations among the German zones broke down by the end of 1945. The country was divided economically as well as politically and ideologically. No agreement could be reached on a German peace treaty. Concerned over the vast amount of material that the Russians were removing from their sector of Germany, Secretary of State Byrnes attempted to counter with a proposal for a unified Germany whose demilitarization would be guaranteed by the four occupying powers (the Big Three plus France). The Soviets rejected this. By the spring of 1946 they had changed their reparation policy—no longer removing machinery from Eastern Germany, but instead producing goods in that zone where labor and resources were more readily available than in Russia. Another step towards a long-term division of Germany was taken in the autumn of 1946 when the United States and Great Britain merged their zones. Later, France joined this merger. The fixed American policy was announced in a major speech at Stuttgart, Germany by Secretary Byrnes in September. American occupation forces would remain in Germany as long as necessary, Byrnes dramatically pledged, but many administrative functions in the American zone would be returned to German hands. For a rousing finale, Byrnes observed that the German–Polish boundary was not yet settled to American satisfaction. This was one of the most potentially explosive political issues in European affairs, and one that Russia and France hoped to keep quiet because of their fears of German resurgence. By thus leaving open the possibility that Germany might someday reclaim those lands in the east, Byrnes did nothing to quiet East European, French, or Russian concern over Germany. Of the several issues involved in the German problem, which does Byrnes see as most important?

 No more USSR looting

SOURCE. *Department of State Bulletin*, **XV**, September 15, 1946, pp. 496–501.

We [in the United States] have learned, whether we like it or not, that we live in one world, from which world we cannot isolate ourselves. We have learned that peace and well-being are indivisible and that our peace and well-being cannot be purchased at the price of the peace or the well-being of any other country.

I hope that the German people will never again make the mistake of believing that because the American people are peace-loving they will sit back hoping for peace if any nation uses force or the threat of force to acquire domination over other peoples and other governments. . . .

The carrying out of the Potsdam Agreement has . . . been obstructed by the failure of the Allied Control Council to take the necessary steps to enable the German economy to function as an economic unit. Essential central German administrative departments have not been established, although they are expressly required by the Potsdam Agreement. . . .

United Economy regardless of zones The United States is firmly of the belief that Germany should be administered as an economic unit and that zonal barriers should be completely obliterated so far as the economic life and activity in Germany are concerned.

The conditions which now exist in Germany make it impossible for industrial production to reach the levels which the occupying powers agreed were essential for a minimum German peacetime economy. Obviously, if the agreed levels of industry are to be reached, we cannot continue to restrict the free exchange of commodities, persons, and ideas throughout Germany. The barriers between the four zones of Germany are far more difficult to surmount than those between normal independent states.

New definition of zones [The time has come when the zonal boundaries should be regarded as defining only the areas to be occupied for security purposes by the armed forces of the occupying powers and not as self-contained economic or political units.]

That was the course of development envisaged by the Potsdam Agreement, and that is the course of development which the American Government intends to follow to the full limit of its authority. It has formally announced that it is its intention to unify the economy of its own zone with any or all of the other zones willing to participate in the unification.

So far only the British Government has agreed to let its zone participate. We deeply appreciate their cooperation. Of course, this policy of unification is not intended to exclude the governments not now willing to join. The unification will be open to them at any time they wish to join.

[We favor the economic unification of Germany. If complete unification cannot be secured, we shall do everything in our power to secure the maximum possible unification.] . .

Similarly, there is urgent need for the setting up of a central German administrative agency for industry and foreign trade. . . .

Germany must be given a chance to export goods in order to import enough to make her economy self-sustaining. Germany is a part of Europe, and recovery in Europe, and particularly in the states adjoining Germany, will be slow indeed if Germany with her great resources of iron and coal is turned into a poorhouse. . . .

The Potsdam Agreement did not provide that there should never be *Return to* a central German government; it merely provided that for the time *Democratic* being there should be no central German government. Certainly this *ideals* only meant that no central government should be established until some sort of democracy was rooted in the soil of Germany and some sense of local responsibility developed. . . .

It is the view of the American Government that the German people throughout Germany, under proper safeguards, should now be given the primary responsibility for the running of their own affairs. . . .

From now on the thoughtful people of the world will judge Allied action in Germany not by Allied promises but by Allied performances. The American Government has supported and will continue to support the necessary measures to de-Nazify and demilitarize Germany, but it does not believe that large armies of foreign soldiers or alien bureaucrats, however well motivated and disciplined, are in the long run the most reliable guardians of another country's democracy.

All that the Allied governments can and should do is to lay down the rules under which German democracy can govern itself. The Allied occupation forces should be limited to the number sufficient to see that those rules are obeyed.

But of course the question for us will be: What force is needed to make certain that Germany does not rearm as it did after the first World War? Our proposal for a treaty with the major powers to enforce for 25 or even 40 years the demilitarization plan finally agreed upon in the peace settlement would have made possible a smaller army of occupation. . . . Unfortunately our proposal for a treaty was not agreed to.

Security forces will probably have to remain in Germany for a long period. I want no misunderstanding. We will not shirk our duty. We are not withdrawing. We are staying here. As long as there is an occupation army in Germany, American armed forces will be part of that occupation army.

The United States favors the early establishment of a provisional German government for Germany. Progress has been made in the American zone in developing local and state self-government in Germany, and the American Government believes similar progress is possible in all zones.

It is the view of the American Government that the provisional government should not be hand-picked by other governments. It should be a German national council composed of the democratically responsible minister presidents or other chief officials of the several states or provinces which have been established in each of the four zones. . . .

The German National Council should also be charged with the preparation of a draft of a federal constitution for Germany which, among other things, should insure the democratic character of the new Germany and the human rights and fundamental freedoms of all its inhabitants. . . .

The Soviets and the Poles suffered greatly at the hands of Hitler's invading armies. As a result of the agreement at Yalta, Poland ceded to the Soviet Union territory east of the Curzon Line. Because of this, Poland asked for revision of her northern and western frontiers. The United States will support a revision of these frontiers in Poland's favor. However, the extent of the area to be ceded to Poland must be determined when the final settlement is agreed upon.

The United States does not feel that it can deny to France, which has been invaded three times by Germany in 70 years, its claim to the Saar territory, whose economy has long been closely linked with France. Of course, if the Saar territory is integrated with France she should readjust her reparation claims against Germany.

Except as here indicated, the United States will not support any encroachment on territory which is indisputably German or any division of Germany which is not genuinely desired by the people concerned. So far as the United States is aware the people of the Ruhr and the Rhineland desire to remain united with the rest of Germany. And the United States is not going to oppose their desire. . . .

The American people want to help the German people to win their way back to an honorable place among the free and peace-loving nations of the world.

CHAPTER VI
ALTERNATIVES AND
CONCLUSIONS, 1946–1947

36 FROM   *Winston Churchill*
The Iron Curtain Speech (March 5, 1946)

By early 1946 the United States confronted a cold war with the Soviet Union instead of the long-expected pleasantries of an American Century. Poland and much of Eastern Europe were under Communist control. German affairs were not settled. Attempts to write peace treaties had failed. In China, a carefully constructed armistice between Nationalist and Communist factions collapsed and civil war again erupted. American and Russian military units nearly confronted one another during a crisis in Iran. Stalin initiated a feverish ideological campaign to eliminate Western influences in Eastern Europe and Russia while deifying himself. Americans, meanwhile, began to search for Communists or other un-American officials who must be to blame for the failure of the American Century to appear in the postwar world.

Proposals for new approaches soon appeared. As noted in Chapter I, Secretary of War Henry Stimson advised President Truman to change the American tack toward Russia in September, 1945, but this advice was not followed. American officials who urged a tough line believed their views to be confirmed on February 9, 1946 when Stalin publicly outlined future Soviet policy. He began his speech with a classic Marxist-Leninist analysis explaining why capitalists powers were in a nearly continuing state of war. He then warned the Russian people that in order to protect themselves against the results of capitalist warfare, they must continue to sacrifice under a new series of five-year plans for the rapid rebuilding of the Soviet economy and the further strengthening of the Red Army. Western officials believed that Stalin was digging in for a long cold war against his former. Allies, and some feared the conflict could quickly turn hot. Supreme Court Justice William Douglas, for example, made the famous remark that Stalin's speech was "The Declaration of World War III."

SOURCE. *Congressional Record*, 79th Cong., 2nd Sess., A 1145–1147.

*A month after Stalin spoke, Winston Churchill appeared at Fulton, Missouri. After
being introduced by President Truman, Churchill indirectly responded to Stalin by
urging the United States and Great Britain to form a partnership and, with the aid
of their atomic monopoly, restore a peaceful, viable world. Churchill was no longer
Prime Minister, but he was the most celebrated Western figure to emerge from the
war. His proposals, however, were too advanced for most Americans in early 1946,
particularly when he insisted that they help restore and protect the British Empire.
Within another year his analysis of the problem, if not all of his solutions, were more
warmly appreciated in Washington.*

*In Chapter I, Secretary of State Cordell Hull, after returning from the Moscow
Conference in 1943, told Congress that in the postwar world the traditional balance
of power approach to international problems should disappear. What is the difference
between Hull's remark in 1943 and Churchill's observation three years later in the
following selection that "the old doctrine of a balance of power is unsound"?*

When American military men approach some serious situation they
are wont to write at the head of their directive the words "Over-all
strategic concept." There is wisdom in this as it leads to clarity of
thought. What, then, is the over-all strategic concept which we should
inscribe today? It is nothing less than the safety and welfare, the
freedom and progress of all the homes and families of all the men and
women in all the lands. . . .

To give security to these countless homes they must be shielded from
the two gaunt marauders—war and tyranny. . . .

A world organization has already been erected for the prime
purpose of preventing war. . . . It would nevertheless be wrong and
imprudent to entrust the secret knowledge or experience of the atomic
bomb, which the United States, Great Britain, and Canada now share,
to the world organization, while it is still in its infancy. It would be
criminal madness to cast it adrift in this still agitated and ununited
world. No one in any country has slept less well in their beds because
this knowledge and the method and the raw materials to apply it are
at present largely retained in American hands. I do not believe we
should all have slept so soundly had the positions been reversed and
some Communist or neo-Fascist state monopolized, for the time
being, these dread agencies. . . .

God has willed that this shall not be, and we have at least a breath-
ing space before this peril has to be encountered, and even then, if
no effort is spared, we should still possess so formidable a superiority
as to impose effective deterrents upon its employment or threat of

employment by others. Ultimately when the essential brotherhood of men is truly embodied and expressed in a world organization, these powers may be confided to it.

I now come to the second danger which threatens the cottage home and ordinary people, namely tyranny. We cannot be blind to the fact that the liberties enjoyed by individual citizens throughout the United States and British Empire are not valid in a considerable number of countries, some of which are very powerful. In these states control is enforced upon the common people by various kinds of all-embracing police governments, to a degree which is overwhelming and contrary to every principle of democracy. . . . It is not our duty at this time, when difficulties are so numerous, to interfere forcibly in the internal affairs of countries whom we have not conquered in war, but we must never cease to proclaim in fearless tones the great principles of freedom and the rights of man, which are the joint inheritance of the English-speaking world and which, through Magna Carta, the Bill of Rights, the habeas corpus, trial by jury, and the English common law find their famous expression in the Declaration of Independence. . . .

So far we are evidently in full agreement. Now, while still pursuing the method of realizing our over-all strategic concept, I come to the crux of what I have traveled here to say. Neither the sure prevention of war, nor the continuous rise of world organization, will be gained without what I have called the fraternal association of the English-speaking peoples. This means a special relationship between the British Commonwealth and Empire and the United States. This is no time for generalities. I will venture to be precise.

Fraternal association requires not only the growing friendship and mutual understanding between our two vast but kindred systems of society but the continuance of the intimate relationships between our military advisers, leading to common study of potential dangers, similarity of weapons and manuals of instruction and interchange of officers and cadets at colleges. It should carry with it the continuance of the present facilities for mutual security by the joint use of all naval and Air Force bases in the possession of either country all over the world. This would perhaps double the mobility of the American Navy and Air Force. It would greatly expand that of the British Empire forces. . . .

The United States already has a permanent defense agreement with the Dominion of Canada, which is so devotedly attached to the British Commonwealth and Empire. This agreement is more effective than many of those which have often been made under formal alliances. This principle should be extended to all the British Commonwealths with full reciprocity. Thus, whatever happens, and thus only, we shall be secure ourselves and able to work together for the high and simple causes that are dear to us and bode no ill to any. Eventually there may come the principle of common citizenship but that we may be content to leave to destiny, whose outstretched arm so many of us can clearly see. . . .

The Dark Ages may return, the Stone Age may return on the gleaming wings of science, and what might now shower immeasurable material blessings upon mankind, may even bring about its total destruction. Beware, I say; time may be short. . . .

From Stettin in the Baltic to Trieste in the Adriatic, an iron curtain has descended across the continent. Behind that line lie all the capitals of the ancient states of central and eastern Europe. Warsaw, Berlin, Prague, Vienna, Budapest, Belgrade, Bucharest, and Sofia, all these famous cities and the populations around them lie in the Soviet sphere and all are subject, in one form or another, not only to Soviet influence but to a very high and increasing measure of control from Moscow. Athens alone, with its immortal glories, is free to decide its future at an election under British, American, and French observation. . . .

However, in a great number of countries, far from the Russian frontiers and throughout the world, Communist fifth columns are established and work in complete unity and absolute obedience to the directions they receive from the Communist center. Except in the British Commonwealth, and in the United States, where communism is in its infancy, the Communist parties or fifth columns constitute a growing challenge and peril to Christian civilization. . . .

On the other hand, I repulse the idea that a new war is inevitable, still more that it is imminent. It is because I am so sure that our fortunes are in our own hands and that we hold the power to save the future, that I feel the duty to speak out now that I have an occasion to do so. I do not believe that Soviet Russia desires war. What they desire is the fruits of war and the indefinite expansion of their power and doctrines. . . .

From what I have seen of our Russian friends and allies during the war, I am convinced that there is nothing they admire so much as strength, and there is nothing for which they have less respect than for military weakness. For that reason the old doctrine of a balance of power is unsound. We cannot afford, if we can help it, to work on narrow margins, offering temptations to a trial of strength. If the western democracies stand together in strict adherence to the principles of the United Nations Charter, their influence for furthering these principles will be immense and no one is likely to molest them. If, however, they become divided or falter in their duty, and if these all-important years are allowed to slip away, then indeed catastrophe may overwhelm us all.

3 7   FROM   *Josef Stalin*
Churchill's Speech is a Call for War on Russia
(March 13, 1946)

> *Churchill's speech brought an angry reply from Stalin. In an interview, the Soviet dictator revealed some motives of Russian policy; his belief in an Anglo-American combination against Russian interests, his fear of Germany, and a view that Eastern Europe under Communist control was "a perfectly logical thing" are particularly notable. On which parts of Churchill's speech does Stalin significantly neglect to comment?*

Question: How do you appraise Mr. Churchill's latest speech in the United States of America?

Answer: I appraise it as a dangerous act, calculated to sow the seeds of dissension among the Allied states and impede their collaboration.

Question: Can it be considered that Mr. Churchill's speech is prejudicial to the cause of peace and security?

Answer: Yes, unquestionably. As a matter of fact, Mr. Churchill now takes the stand of the warmongers, and in this Mr. Churchill is not alone. He has friends not only in Britain but in the United States of America as well.

A point to be noted is that in this respect Mr. Churchill and his friends bear a striking resemblance to Hitler and his friends. Hitler began his work of unleashing war by proclaiming a race theory, declaring that only German-speaking people constituted a superior

SOURCE. Interview with correspondent of Soviet newspaper *Pravda*, March 13, 1946.

nation. Mr. Churchill sets out to unleash war with a race theory, asserting that only English-speaking nations are superior nations, who are called upon to decide the destinies of the entire world. The German race theory led Hitler and his friends to the conclusion that the Germans, as the only superior nation, should rule over other nations. The English race theory leads Mr. Churchill and his friends to the conclusion that the English-speaking nations, as the only superior nations, should rule over the rest of the nations of the world.

Actually, Mr. Churchill, and his friends in Britain and the United States, present to the non-English-speaking nations something in the nature of an ultimatum: "Accept our rule voluntarily, and then all will be well; otherwise war is inevitable."

But the nations shed their blood in the course of five years' fierce war for the sake of the liberty and independence of their countries, and not in order to exchange the domination of the Hitlers for the domination of the Churchills. It is quite probable, accordingly, that the non-English-speaking nations, which constitute the vast majority of the population of the world, will not agree to submit to a new slavery.

It is Mr. Churchill's tragedy that, inveterate Tory that he is, he does not understand this simple and obvious truth.

There can be no doubt that Mr. Churchill's position is a war position, a call for war on the U.S.S.R. It is also clear that this position of Mr. Churchill's is incompatible with the Treaty of Alliance existing between Britain and the U.S.S.R. True, Mr. Churchill does say, in passing, in order to confuse his readers, that the term of the Anglo-Soviet Treaty of Mutual Assistance and Collaboration might quite well be extended to fifty years. But how is such a statement on Mr. Churchill's part to be reconciled with his position of war on the U.S.S.R., with his preaching of war against the U.S.S.R.? Obviously, these things cannot be reconciled by any means whatever. And if Mr. Churchill, who calls for war on the Soviet Union, at the same time considers it possible to extend the term of the Anglo-Soviet Treaty to fifty years, that means that he regards this treaty as a mere scrap of paper, which he only needs in order to disguise and camouflage his anti-Soviet position. . . .

Question: How do you appraise the part of Mr. Churchill's speech in which he attacks the democratic systems in the European states bordering upon us, and criticizes the good neighborly relations established between these states and the Soviet Union?

Answer: This part of Mr. Churchill's speech is compounded of elements of slander and elements of discourtesy and tactlessness. Mr. Churchill asserts that "Warsaw, Berlin, Prague, Vienna, Budapest, Belgrade, Bucharest, Sofia—all these famous cities and the populations around them—lie within the Soviet sphere and are all subject in one form or another not only to Soviet influence, but to a very high and increasing measure of control from Moscow." Mr. Churchill describes all this as "unlimited expansionist tendencies" on the part of the Soviet Union.

It needs no particular effort to show that in this Mr. Churchill grossly and unceremoniously slanders both Moscow and the above-named states bordering on the U.S.S.R.

In the first place it is quite absurd to speak of exclusive control by the U.S.S.R. in Vienna and Berlin, where there are Allied Control Councils made up of the representatives of four states and where the U.S.S.R. has only one-quarter of the votes. It does happen that some people cannot help engaging in slander. But still, there is a limit to everything.

Secondly, the following circumstances should not be forgotten. The Germans made their invasion of the U.S.S.R. through Finland, Poland, Rumania, Bulgaria, and Hungary. The Germans were able to make their invasion through these countries because, at the time, governments hostile to the Soviet Union existed in these countries. As a result of the German invasion the Soviet Union has lost irretrievably in the fighting against the Germans, and also through the German occupation and the deportation of Soviet citizens to German servitude, a total of about seven million people. In other words, the Soviet Union's loss of life has been several times greater than that of Britain and the United States of America put together. Possibly in some quarters an inclination is felt to forget about these colossal sacrifices of the Soviet people which secured the liberation of Europe from the Hitlerite yoke. But the Soviet Union cannot forget about them. And so what can there be surprising about the fact that the Soviet Union, anxious for its future safety, is trying to see to it that governments loyal in their attitude to the Soviet Union should exist in these countries? How can anyone, who has not taken leave of his wits, describe these peaceful aspirations of the Soviet Union as expansionist tendencies on the part of our state?

... Mr. Churchill is displeased that Poland has faced about in her policy in the direction of friendship and alliance with the U.S.S.R. There was a time when elements of conflict and antagonism predominated in the relations between Poland and the U.S.S.R. This circumstance enabled statesmen like Mr. Churchill to play on these antagonisms, to get control over Poland on the pretext of protecting her from the Russians, to try to scare Russia with the specter of war between herself and Poland, and retain the position of arbiter for themselves. But that time is past and gone, for the enmity between Poland and Russia has given way to friendship between them, and Poland—present-day democratic Poland—does not choose to be a football in foreign hands any longer. . . .

As to Mr. Churchill's attack upon the Soviet Union in connection with the extension of Poland's western frontier to include Polish territories which the Germans had seized in the past—here it seems to me he is plainly cheating. As is known, the decision on the western frontier of Poland was adopted at the Berlin Three-Power Conference [the Potsdam Conference of July, 1945] on the basis of Poland's demands. The Soviet Union has repeatedly stated that it considers Poland's demands to be proper and just. It is quite probable that Mr. Churchill is displeased with this decision. But why does Mr. Churchill, while sparing no shots against the Russian position in this matter, conceal from his readers the fact that this decision was passed at the Berlin Conference by unanimous vote—that it was not only the Russians but the British and Americans as well who voted for the decision? Why did Mr. Churchill think it necessary to mislead the public? . . . As is known, the government of the state in Britain at the present time is in the hands of one party, the Labor Party, and the opposition parties are deprived of the right to participate in the government of Britain. That Mr. Churchill calls true democracy. Poland, Romania, Yugoslavia, Bulgaria, and Hungary are administered by blocs of several parties—from four to six parties—and the opposition, if it is more or less loyal, is secured the right of participation in the government. That Mr. Churchill describes as totalitarianism, tyranny, and police rule. Why? On what grounds? Don't expect a reply from Mr. Churchill. . . .

Mr. Churchill comes somewhere near the truth when he speaks of the increasing influence of the Communist parties in eastern Europe. It must be remarked, however, that he is not quite accurate. The influence of the Communist parties has grown not only in eastern Europe, but in nearly all the countries of Europe which were previously under fascist rule—Italy, Germany, Hungary, Bulgaria, Romania, and Finland—or which experienced German, Italian, or Hungarian   occupation—France,   Belgium,   Holland,   Norway,

Denmark, Poland, Czechoslovakia, Yugoslavia, Greece, the Soviet Union and so on.

The increased influence of the Communists cannot be considered fortuitous. It is a perfectly logical thing. The influence of the Communists has grown because, in the years of the rule of fascism in Europe, the Communists showed themselves trusty, fearless, self-sacrificing fighters against the fascist regime for the liberty of the peoples. . . . These plain people have views of their own, a policy of their own, and they know how to stand up for themselves. It was they, the millions of these plain people, who defeated Mr. Churchill and his party in Britain by casting their votes for the Laborites. It was they, the millions of these plain people, who isolated the reactionaries and advocates of collaboration with fascism in Europe, and gave their preference to the Left democratic parties. It was they, the millions of these plain people, who after testing the Communists in the fires of struggle and resistance to fascism, came to the conclusion that the Communists were fully deserving of the people's confidence. That was how the influence of the Communists grew in Europe.

Of course Mr. Churchill does not like this course of development and he sounds the alarm and appeals to force. But neither did he like the birth of the Soviet regime in Russia after the First World War. At that time, too, he sounded the alarm and organized an armed campaign of fourteen states against Russia setting himself the goal of turning back the wheel of history. But history proved stronger than the Churchill intervention, and Mr. Churchill's quixotry led to his unmitigated defeat at that time. I don't know whether Mr. Churchill and his friends will succeed in organizing a new armed campaign against eastern Europe after the Second World War; but if they do succeed—which is not very probable because millions of plain people stand guard over the cause of peace—it may confidently be said that they will be thrashed, just as they were thrashed once before, twenty-six years ago.

38   FROM   *Henry Wallace*
     The Tougher We Get, the Tougher the Russians
            Will Get (September 12, 1946)

Secretary of Commerce Henry Wallace was particularly disturbed by Churchill's speech at Fulton, Missouri. One of the foremost of the Roosevelt New Dealers, Wallace had served as Secretary of Agriculture, Vice-President, and finally as Secretary of Commerce under Roosevelt. Troubled about those whom he liked to call the "Common Man," Wallace was deeply concerned about maintaining American prosperity and social stability through increased aid to small business and especially by vastly increasing foreign trade. During the last years of the war he constantly reiterated the need for Americans to find more markets abroad if they were to escape a replay of the 1930s depression. He had agreed with Henry Morgenthau, Jr., that the United States would have to work closely with Russia for reciprocal economic benefits. The course of postwar foreign policy therefore frightened Wallace. Throughout the first half of 1946, the Secretary of Commerce challenged Truman's foreign policies privately. On September 12, 1946, at a political rally in New York, Wallace made his fears public. For his efforts, Secretary of State Byrnes demanded that Truman fire Wallace. On September 20, Wallace retired to farming in upstate New York. But shortly thereafter, he became the focal point of a political movement which aimed to defeat Truman in the 1948 elections and reverse American policies. That attempt, of course, also failed. In view of the September, 1946 speech, which follows, is it accurate to characterize Wallace as a "radical"?

. . . The price of peace—for us and for every nation in the world—is the price of giving up prejudice, hatred, fear, and ignorance.

Let's get down to cases here at home.

First we have prejudice, hatred, fear and ignorance of certain races. The recent mass lynching in Georgia was not merely the most unwarranted, brutal act of mob violence in the United States in recent years; it was also an illustration of the kind of prejudice that makes war inevitable.

Hatred breeds hatred. The doctrine of racial superiority produces a desire to get even on the part of its victims. If we are to work for peace in the rest of the world, we here in the United States must eliminate racism from our unions, our business organizations, our educational institutions, and our employment practices. Merit alone must be the measure of man.

SOURCE. *Vital Speeches of the Day*, XII, October 1, 1946, pp. 738–741. Reprinted by permission.

Second, in payment for peace, we must give up prejudice, hatred, fear and ignorance in the economic world. This means working earnestly, day after day, for a larger volume of world trade. It means helping undeveloped areas of the world to industrialize themselves with the help of American technical assistance and loans.

We should welcome the opportunity to help along the most rapid possible industrialization in Latin America, China, India, and the Near East. For as the productivity of these people increases, our exports will increase. . . .

Governor Dewey [Thomas E. Dewey of New York] has expressed himself as favoring an alliance of mutual defense with Great Britain as the key to our foreign policy. This may sound attractive because we both speak the same language and many of our customs and traditions have the same historical background. Moreover, to the military men, the British Isles are our advanced air base against Europe.

Certainly we like the British people as individuals. But to make Fear of Britain the key to our foreign policy would be, in my opinion, the US-Br height of folly. We must not let the reactionary leadership of the alliance Republican party force us into that position. We must not let British balance-of-power manipulations determine whether and when the United States gets into war.

Make no mistake about it—the British imperialistic policy in the Near East alone, combined with Russian retaliation, would lead the United States straight to war unless we have a clearly-defined and realistic policy of our own. . . .

In this connection, I want one thing clearly understood. I am neither anti-British nor pro-British—neither anti-Russian nor pro-Russian. And just two days ago, when President Truman read these words, he said that they represented the policy of his administration.

I plead for an America vigorously dedicated to peace—just as I plead for opportunities for the next generation throughout the world to enjoy the abundance which now, more than ever before, is the birthright of men.

To achieve lasting peace, we must study in detail just how the Russian character was formed—by invasions of Tartars, Mongols, Germans, Poles, Swedes, and French; by the intervention of the British, French and Americans in Russian affairs from 1919 to 1921; by the geography of the huge Russian land mass situated strategically between Europe and Asia; and by the vitality derived from the rich Russian soil and the strenuous Russian climate. Add to all this the tremendous emotional power which Marxism and Leninism gives to the Russian leaders—and then we can realize that we are reckoning with a force which cannot be handled successfully by a "Get tough with Russia" policy. "Getting tough" never bought anything real and lasting—whether for schoolyard bullies or businessmen or world powers. The tougher we get, the tougher the Russians will get. . . .

We must not let our Russian policy be guided or influenced by those inside or outside the United States who want war with Russia. This does not mean appeasement.

We most earnestly want peace with Russia—but we want to be met half way. We want cooperation. And I believe that we can get cooperation once Russia understands that our primary objective is neither saving the British Empire nor purchasing oil in the Near East with the lives of American soldiers. We cannot allow national oil rivalries to force us into war. All the nations producing oil, whether inside or outside of their own boundaries, must fulfill the provisions of the United Nations Charter and encourage the development of world petroleum reserves so as to make the maximum amount of oil available to all nations of the world on an equitable peaceful basis— and not on the basis of fighting the next war.

For her part, Russia can retain our respect by cooperating with the United Nations in a spirit of openminded and flexible give-and-take.

The real peace treaty we now need is between the United States and Russia. On our part, we should recognize that we have no more business in the *political* affairs of Eastern Europe than Russia has in the *political* affairs of Latin America, Western Europe and the United States. We may not like what Russia does in Eastern Europe. Her type of land reform, industrial expropriation, and suppression of basic liberties offends the great majority of the people of the United States. But whether we like it or not the Russians will try to socialize their sphere of influence just as we try to democratize our sphere of influence. . . .

We know what Russia is up to in Eastern Europe, for example, and Russia knows what we are up to. We cannot permit the door to be closed against our trade in Eastern Europe any more than we can in China. But at the same time we have to recognize that the Balkans are closer to Russia than to us—and that Russia cannot permit either England or the United States to dominate the politics of that area.

China is a special case and although she holds the longest frontier in the world with Russia, the interests of world peace demand that China remain free from any sphere of influence, either politically or economically. We insist that the door to trade and economic development opportunities be left wide open in China as in all the world. However, the open door to trade and opportunities for economic development in China are meaningless unless there is a unified and peaceful China—built on the cooperation of the various groups in that country and based on a hands-off policy of the outside powers.

We are still arming to the hilt. Our excessive expenses for military purposes are the chief cause for our unbalanced budget. If taxes are to be lightened we must have the basis of a real peace with Russia— a peace that cannot be broken by extremist propagandists. We do not want our course determined for us by master minds operating out of London, Moscow or Nanking.

Russian ideas of social-economic justice are going to govern nearly a third of the world. Our ideas of free enterprise democracy will govern much of the rest. The two ideas will endeavor to prove which can deliver the most satisfaction to the common man in their respective areas of political dominance. But by mutual agreement, this competition should be put on a friendly basis and the Russians should stop conniving against us in certain areas of the world just as we should stop scheming against them in other parts of the world. Let the results of the two systems speak for themselves.

Meanwhile, the Russians should stop teaching that their form of communism must, by force if necessary, ultimately triumph over democratic capitalism—while we should close our ears to those among us who would have us believe that Russian communism and our free enterprise system cannot live, one with another, in a profitable and productive peace.

[Under friendly peaceful competition the Russian world and the American world will gradually become more alike. The Russians will be forced to grant more and more of the personal freedoms; and we shall become more and more absorbed with the problems of social-economic justice.]

Russia must be convinced that we are not planning for war against her and we must be certain that Russia is not carrying on territorial expansion or world domination through native communists faithfully following every twist and turn in the Moscow party line. But in this competition, we must insist on an open door for trade throughout the world. There will always be an ideological conflict—but that is

no reason why diplomats cannot work out a basis for both systems
to live safely in the world side by side. . . .

In brief, as I see it today, the World Order is bankrupt—and the
United States, Russia, and England are the receivers.

39   FROM   *Harry S. Truman:*
The Freedoms of Worship and Speech are Related to Freedom of
Enterprise (March 6, 1947)

*Henry Wallace's speech of September, 1946 was little more than a glaring exception
in the consensus that was developing around the foreign policy of the Truman Administration. In March 1947, one of the more significant months in American diplomatic
history, President Truman publicly defined and committed his Administration to a
series of policies that shaped American foreign policy for at least the next twenty years.
The immediate reason for Truman's action was the private information imparted by
the British Ambassador in Washington to the Department of State in January 1947,
that the British Empire could no longer support the Greek government in its fight
against Communist-led insurgents. Until early 1947, the United States policy in
dealing with such conflicts had not been broadly defined. It now seems fair to say
that the Administration had been watching the Greek situation closely for more than
a year, merely waiting for the appropriate moment to throw its full weight behind
the formal government. The British plea of imminent bankruptcy provided the opportunity. In two remarkable speeches made within the same week in March, President
Truman defined the American mission. The first speech, which attracted relatively little
attention, is given in the following selection. In this address at Baylor University,
the President gave one of the most explicit explanations of the relationship between
politics and economics, the ties between domestic and foreign policies, and the differences
between freedom and totalitarianism that any President, or any other public official, has
offered. This speech formed the preface for the famous Truman Doctrine speech which
followed six days later. The Soviet Union is not directly mentioned in the March 6
speech, but since its trade is entirely controlled by a Soviet government agency, what
are the implications of President Truman's words for Russian–American relations?*

. . . At this particular time, the whole world is concentrating much
of its thought and energy on attaining the objectives of peace and freedom. These objectives are bound up completely with a third objective—

SOURCE. *Public Papers of the Presidents . . . Harry S. Truman . . . 1947*, Washington,
D.C.: Government Printing Office, 1963, pp. 167–172.

reestablishment of world trade. In fact the three—peace, freedom, and world trade—are inseparable. The grave lessons of the past have proved it.

Many of our people, here in America, used to think that we could escape the troubles of the world by simply staying within our own borders. Two wars have shown how wrong they were. We know today that we cannot find security in isolation. If we are to live at peace, we must join with other nations in a continuing effort to organize the world for peace. Science and invention have left us no other alternative. . . .

But some among us do not fully realize what we must do to carry out this policy. There still are those who seem to believe that we can confine our cooperation with other countries to political relationships; that we need not cooperate where economic questions are involved.

This attitude has sometimes led to the assertion that there should be bipartisan support for the foreign policy of the United States, but that there need not be bipartisan support for the foreign *economic* policy of the United States.

Such a statement simply does not make sense.

Our foreign relations, political and economic, are indivisible. We cannot say that we are willing to cooperate in the one field and are unwilling to cooperate in the other. I am glad to note that the leaders in both parties have recognized that fact. . . .

We are the giant of the economic world. Whether we like it or not, the future pattern of economic relations depends upon us. The world is waiting and watching to see what we shall do. The choice is ours. We can lead the nations to economic peace or we can plunge them into economic war.

There must be no question as to our course. We must not go through the thirties again.

There is abundant evidence, I think, that these earlier mistakes will not be repeated. We have already made a good start. Our Government has participated fully in setting up, under the United Nations, agencies of international cooperation for dealing with relief and refugees, with food and agriculture, with shipping and aviation, with loans for reconstruction and development, and with the stabilization of currencies . . . .

There is one thing that Americans value even more than peace. It is freedom. Freedom of worship—freedom of speech—freedom of enterprise. It must be true that the first two of these freedoms are related to the third. For, throughout history, freedom of worship and freedom of speech have been most frequently enjoyed in those societies that have accorded a considerable measure of freedom to individual enterprise. Freedom has flourished where power has been dispersed. It has languished where power has been too highly centralized. So our devotion to freedom of enterprise, in the United States, has deeper roots than a desire to protect the profits of ownership. It is part and parcel of what we call American.

The pattern of international trade that is most conducive to freedom of enterprise is one in which the major decisions are made, not by governments, but by private buyers and sellers, under conditions of active competition, and with proper safeguards against the establishment of monopolies and cartels. Under such a system, buyers make their purchases, and sellers make their sales, at whatever time and place and in whatever quantities they choose, relying for guidance on whatever prices the market may afford. Goods move from country to country in response to economic opportunities. Governments may impose tariffs, but they do not dictate the quantity of trade, the sources of imports, or the destination of exports. Individual transactions are a matter of private choice.

This is the essence of free enterprise.

The pattern of trade that is *least* conducive to freedom of enterprise is one in which decisions are made by governments. Under such a system, the quantity of purchases and sales, the sources of imports, and the destination of exports are dictated by public officials. In some cases, trade may be conducted by the state. In others, part or all of it may be left in private hands. But, even so, the trader is not free. Governments make all the important choices and he adjusts himself to them as best he can.

This was the pattern of the seventeenth and eighteenth centuries. Unless we act, and act decisively, it will be the pattern of the next century.

Everywhere on earth, nations are under economic pressure. Countries that were devastated by the war are seeking to reconstruct their industries. Their need to import, in the months that lie ahead, will exceed their capacity to export. And so they feel that imports must be rigidly controlled.

Countries that have lagged in their development are seeking to industrialize. In order that new industries may be established, they, too, feel that competing imports must be rigidly controlled. . . .

If this trend is not reversed, the Government of the United

States will be under pressure, sooner or later, to use these same devices to fight for markets and for raw materials. And if the Government were to yield to this pressure, it would shortly find itself in the business of allocating foreign goods among importers and foreign markets among exporters and telling every trader what he could buy or sell, and how much, and when, and where. This is precisely what we have been trying to get away from, as rapidly as possible, ever since the war. It is not the American way. It is not the way to peace. . . .

The size of our market is not forever fixed. It is smaller when we attempt to isolate ourselves from the other countries of the world. It is larger when we have a thriving foreign trade. Our imports were down to a billion dollars in 1932; they were up to five billion in 1946. But no one would contend that 1932 was a better year than 1946 for selling goods, or making profits, or finding jobs. Business is poor when markets are small. Business is good when markets are big. It is the purpose of the coming negotiations to lower existing barriers to trade so that markets everywhere may grow. . . .

40   FROM   *Harry S. Truman*
          The Truman Doctrine (March 12, 1947)

The speech at Baylor University on March 6 by President Truman was a restatement of some of the terms of Luce's American Century and a recapitulation of the economic beliefs that had guided American policy makers as they formulated postwar plans. But it also served as an introduction for the Truman Doctrine speech delivered to Congress on March 12. That famous speech is given in the next selection. Perhaps the most striking feature of the speech is the sharpness with which the President divides the world. Senator Arthur Vandenberg of Michigan, leader of the Republicans in the Senate Foreign Relations Committee, had advised President Truman to "scare hell" out of the American people in order to get support for the Doctrine. The President did this so effectively that Congress quickly passed the aid appropriations for Greece and Turkey. The tone of the message, the President's definition of the threats posed by "aggressive movements," and the later labeling of the speech as a "doctrine" are especially important. Is the Truman Doctrine speech a summary of the previous several years of American foreign policy, or did it mark a new departure?

SOURCE. *Public Papers of the Presidents . . . Harry S. Truman . . . 1947*, Washington, D.C.: Government Printing Office, 1963, pp. 176–180.

Mr. President, Mr. Speaker, Members of the Congress of the United States:

The gravity of the situation which confronts the world today necessitates my appearance before a joint session of the Congress.

The foreign policy and the national security of this country are involved.

One aspect of the present situation, which I wish to present to you at this time for your consideration and decision, concerns Greece and Turkey.

The United States has received from the Greek Government an urgent appeal for financial and economic assistance. Preliminary reports from the American Economic Mission now in Greece and reports from the American Ambassador in Greece corroborate the statement of the Greek Government that assistance is imperative if Greece is to survive as a free nation.

I do not believe that the American people and the Congress wish to turn a deaf ear to the appeal of the Greek Government.

Greece is not a rich country. Lack of sufficient natural resources has always forced the Greek people to work hard to make both ends meet. Since 1940 this industrious and peace-loving country has suffered invasion, four years of cruel enemy occupation, and bitter internal strife. . . .

Ideology strong

The very existence of the Greek state is today threatened by the terrorist activities of several thousand armed men, led by Communists, who defy the Government's authority at a number of points, particularly along the northern boundaries. A commission appointed by the United Nations Security Council is at present investigating disturbed conditions in northern Greece and alleged border violations along the frontier between Greece on the one hand and Albania, Bulgaria, and Yugoslavia on the other.

Meanwhile, the Greek Government is unable to cope with the situation. The Greek Army is small and poorly equipped. It needs supplies and equipment if it is to restore authority to the Government throughout Greek territory.

Greece must have assistance if it is to become a self-supporting

Military Aid?

and self-respecting democracy.

The United States must supply that assistance. We have already extended to Greece certain types of relief and economic aid, but these are inadequate.

There is no other country to which democratic Greece can turn.

No other nation is willing and able to provide the necessary support for a democratic Greek Government.

The British Government, which has been helping Greece, can give *Fall of Br.* no further financial or economic aid after March 31. Great Britain *as controlling* finds itself under the necessity of reducing or liquidating its com- *power* mitments in several parts of the world, including Greece.

We have considered how the United Nations might assist in this crisis. But the situation is an urgent one requiring immediate action, and the United Nations and its related organizations are not in a position to extend help of the kind that is required.

It is important to note that the Greek Government has asked for our aid in utilizing effectively the financial and other assistance we may give to Greece, and in improving its public administration. It is of the utmost importance that we supervise the use of any funds made available to Greece, in such a manner that each dollar spent will count toward making Greece self-supporting, and will help to build an economy in which a healthy democracy can flourish.

No government is perfect. One of the chief virtues of a democracy, however, is that its defects are always visible and under democratic processes can be pointed out and corrected. The Government of Greece is not perfect. Nevertheless it represents 85 percent of the members of the Greek Parliament who were chosen in an election last year. Foreign observers, including 692 Americans, considered this election to be a fair expression of the views of the Greek people.

The Greek Government has been operating in an atmosphere of chaos and extremism. It has made mistakes. The extension of aid by this country does not mean that the United States condones everything that the Greek Government has done or will do. We have condemned in the past, and we condemn now, extremist measures of the right or the left. We have in the past advised tolerance, and we advise tolerance now.

Greece's neighbor, Turkey, also deserves our attention.

The future of Turkey as an independent and economically sound state is clearly no less important to the freedom-loving peoples of the world than the future of Greece. The circumstances in which Turkey finds itself today are considerably different from those of Greece. Turkey has been spared the disasters that have beset Greece. And during the war the United States and Great Britain furnished Turkey with material aid.

Nevertheless, Turkey now needs our support.

Since the war Turkey has sought additional financial assistance from

Great Britain and the United States for the purpose of effecting that modernization necessary for the maintenance of its national integrity.

That integrity is essential to the preservation of order in the Middle East.

The British Government has informed us that, owing to its own difficulties, it can no longer extend financial or economic aid to Turkey.

As in the case of Greece, if Turkey is to have the assistance it needs, the United States must supply it. We are the only country able to provide that help.

I am fully aware of the broad implications involved if the United States aids in the creation of conditions in which we and other nations will be able to work out a way of life free from coercion. This was a fundamental issue in the war with Germany and Japan. Our victory was won over countries which sought to impose their will, and their way of life upon other nations.

To insure the peaceful development of nations, free from coercion, the United States has taken a leading part in establishing the United Nations. The United Nations is designed to make possible lasting freedom and independence for all its members. We shall not realize our objectives, however, unless we are willing to help free peoples to maintain their free institutions and their national integrity against aggressive movements that seek to impose upon them totalitarian regimes. This is no more than a frank recognition that totalitarian regimes imposed upon free peoples, by direct or indirect aggression, undermine the foundations of international peace and hence the security of the United States.

The peoples of a number of countries of the world have recently had totalitarian regimes forced upon them against their will. The Government of the United States has made frequent protests against coercion and intimidation, in violation of the Yalta agreement, in Poland, Rumania, and Bulgaria. I must also state that in a number of other countries there have been similar developments.

At the present moment in world history nearly every nation must choose between alternative ways of life. The choice is too often not a free one.

One way of life is based upon the will of the majority, and is distinguished by free institutions, representative government, free elections, guaranties of individual liberty, freedom of speech and religion, and freedom from political oppression.

The second way of life is based upon the will of a minority forcibly imposed upon the majority. It relies upon terror and oppression, a controlled press and radio, fixed elections, and the suppression of personal freedoms.

I believe that it must be the policy of the United States to support free peoples who are resisting attempted subjugation by armed minorities or by outside pressures.

I believe that we must assist free peoples to work out their own destinies in their own way.   *Not military involved*

I believe that our help should be primarily through economic and financial aid which is essential to economic stability and orderly political processes.

The world is not static, and the *status quo* is not sacred. But we cannot allow changes in the *status quo* in violation of the Charter of the United Nations by such methods as coercion, or by such subterfuges as political infiltration. In helping free and independent nations to maintain their freedom, the United States will be giving effect to the principles of the Charter of the United Nations.   *US champion liberty + freedom*

It is necessary only to glance at a map to realize that the survival and integrity of the Greek nation are of grave importance in a much wider situation. If Greece should fall under the control of an armed minority, the effect upon its neighbor, Turkey, would be immediate and serious. Confusion and disorder might well spread throughout the entire Middle East.

Moreover, the disappearance of Greece as an independent state would have a profound effect upon those countries in Europe whose peoples are struggling against great difficulties to maintain their freedoms and their independence while they repair the damages of war.

It would be an unspeakable tragedy if these countries, which have struggled so long against overwhelming odds, should lose that victory for which they sacrificed so much. Collapse of free institutions and loss of independence would be disastrous not only for them but for the world. Discouragement and possibly failure would quickly be the lot of neighboring peoples striving to maintain their freedom and independence.

Should we fail to aid Greece and Turkey in this fateful hour, the effect will be far-reaching to the West as well as to the East.

We must take immediate and resolute action.

I therefore ask the Congress to provide authority for assistance to Greece and Turkey in the amount of $400,000,000 for the period ending June 30, 1948. In requesting these funds, I have taken into consideration the maximum amount of relief assistance which would be furnished to Greece out of the $350,000,000 which I recently requested that the Congress authorize for the prevention of starvation and suffering in countries devastated by the war.

military
advisor

In addition to funds, I ask the Congress to authorize the detail of American civilian and military personnel to Greece and Turkey, at the request of those countries, to assist in the tasks of reconstruction, and for the purpose of supervising the use of such financial and material assistance as may be furnished. I recommend that authority also be provided for the instruction and training of selected Greek and Turkish personnel.

Finally, I ask that the Congress provide authority which will permit the speediest and most effective use, in terms of needed commodities, supplies, and equipment, of such funds as may be authorized.

If further funds, or further authority, should be needed for purposes indicated in this message, I shall not hesitate to bring the situation before the Congress. On this subject the Executive and Legislative branches of the Government must work together.

This is a serious course upon which we embark.

I would not recommend it except that the alternative is much more serious.

The United States contributed $341,000,000,000 toward winning World War II. This is an investment in world freedom and world peace.

The assistance that I am recommending for Greece and Turkey amounts to little more than one-tenth of one percent of this investment. It is only common sense that we should safeguard this investment and make sure that it was not in vain.

The seeds of totalitarian regimes are nurtured by misery and want. They spread and grow in the evil soil of poverty and strife. They reach their full growth when the hope of a people for a better life has died.

We must keep that hope alive.

The free peoples of the world look to us for support in maintaining their freedoms.

If we falter in our leadership, we may endanger the peace of the world—and we shall surely endanger the welfare of our own Nation.

Great responsibilities have been placed upon us by the swift movement of events.

I am confident that the Congress will face these responsibilities squarely.

41 FROM *Secretary of State George C. Marshall*
The Marshall Plan (June 15, 1947)

The American mission, as defined by President Truman on March 6 and 12, knew few restraints or boundaries. During the same weeks that the Doctrine was created, however, the State Department was focusing its attention on conditions in Western Europe. War devastation and several winters that were among the coldest in memory had drained resources and prevented rapid recuperation. Washington officials also feared that unless the situation improved, discontented voters might put Communists in power in Italy and France. The continued prosperity of the United States, moreover, depended on fully reopening its traditional trade channels with a healthy Europe. American exports were nearly $16 billion annually in early 1947, but European exports to the United States were less than half that amount, and Europe did not have enough dollars to pay the difference. The United States had to extend dollar and material aid quickly or Europeans would not be able to buy the American goods needed to rebuild their economy. After nearly three months of intensive preparations, Secretary of State George C. Marshall outlined an American proposal at the Harvard Commencement exercises on June 5, 1947. He urged Europeans to take the initiative in formulating a long-term plan, and he did not exclude participation by the Soviets. Sixteen European nations responded by meeting throughout the summer and offering a plan to the United States. After several days of exploring the possibilities of the plan, the Soviets refused to participate. In April, 1948 Congress created the Economic Cooperation Administration which handled the Marshall Plan aid. Over a four-year period, the United States appropriated approximately $12 billion, plus another $1 billion for assistance on credit terms, to Western Europe for economic rebuilding. Does the Marshall Plan have precedents in American planning in 1944–1945 for the postwar world?

I need not tell you gentlemen that the world situation is very serious. That must be apparent to all intelligent people. I think one difficulty is that the problem is one of such enormous complexity that the very mass of facts presented to the public by press and radio make it exceedingly difficult for the man in the street to reach a clear appraisement of the situation. Furthermore, the people of this country are distant from the troubled areas of the earth and it is hard for them to comprehend the plight and consequent reactions of the long-suffering peoples, and the effect of those reactions on their governments in connection with our efforts to promote peace in the world.

SOURCE. *Department of State Bulletin*, **XVI**, June 15, 1947, pp. 1159–1160.

Humanitarian Appeal

In considering the requirements for the rehabilitation of Europe, the physical loss of life, the visible destruction of cities, factories, mines, and railroads was correctly estimated, but it has become obvious during recent months that this visible destruction was probably less serious than the dislocation of the entire fabric of European economy. For the past 10 years conditions have been highly abnormal. The feverish preparation for war and the more feverish maintenance of the war effort engulfed all aspects of national economies. Machinery has fallen into disrepair or is entirely obsolete. Under the arbitrary and destructive Nazi rule, virtually every possible enterprise was geared into the German war machine. Long-standing commercial ties, private institutions, banks, insurance companies, and shipping companies disappeared, through loss of capital, absorption through nationalization, or by simple destruction. In many countries, confidence in the local currency has been severely shaken. The breakdown of the business structure of Europe during the war was complete. Recovery has been seriously retarded by the fact that two years after the close of hostilities a peace settlement with Germany and Austria has not been agreed upon. But even given a more prompt solution of these difficult problems, the rehabilitation of the economic structure of Europe quite evidently will require a much longer time and greater effort than had been foreseen.

There is a phase of this matter which is both interesting and serious. The farmer has always produced the foodstuffs to exchange with the city dweller for the other necessities of life. This division of labor is the basis of modern civilization. At the present time it is threatened with breakdown. . . .

The truth of the matter is that Europe's requirements for the next 3 or 4 years of foreign food and other essential products—principally from America—are so much greater than her present ability to pay that she must have substantial additional help or face economic, social, and political deterioration of a very grave character.

The remedy lies in breaking the vicious circle and restoring the confidence of the European people in the economic future of their own countries and of Europe as a whole. The manufacturer and the farmer throughout wide areas must be able and willing to exchange their products for currencies the continuing value of which is not open to question.

Aside from the demoralizing effect on the world at large and the possibilities of disturbances arising as a result of the desperation of the people concerned, the consequences to the economy of the

United States should be apparent to all. It is logical that the United States should do whatever it is able to do to assist in the return of normal economic health in the world, without which there can be no political stability and no assured peace. Our policy is directed not against any country or doctrine but against hunger, poverty, desperation, and chaos. Its purpose should be the revival of a working economy in the world so as to permit the emergence of political and social conditions in which free institutions can exist. Such assistance, I am convinced, must not be on a piecemeal basis as various crises develop. Any assistance that this Government may render in the future should provide a cure rather than a mere palliative. Any government that is willing to assist in the task of recovery will find full cooperation, I am sure, on the part of the United States Government. Any government which maneuvers to block the recovery of other countries cannot expect help from us. Furthermore, governments, political parties, or groups which seek to perpetuate human misery in order to profit therefrom politically or otherwise will encounter the opposition of the United States.

It is already evident that, before the United States Government can proceed much further in its efforts to alleviate the situation and help start the European world on its way to recovery, there must be some agreement among the countries of Europe as to the requirements of the situation and the part those countries themselves will take in order to give proper effect to whatever action might be undertaken by this Government. It would be neither fitting nor efficacious for this Government to undertake to draw up unilaterally a program designed to place Europe on its feet economically. This is the business of the Europeans. The initiative, I think, must come from Europe. The role of this country should consist of friendly aid in the drafting of a European program and of later support of such a program so far as it may be practical for us to do so. The program should be a joint one, agreed to by a number, if not all, European nations.

An essential part of any successful action on the part of the United States is an understanding on the part of the people of America of the character of the problem and the remedies to be applied. Political passion and prejudice should have no part. With foresight, and a willingness on the part of our people to face up to the vast responsibility which history has clearly placed upon our country, the difficulties I have outlined can and will be overcome.

42   FROM   *Andrei Vyshinsky*
          A Soviet Criticism of the Truman Doctrine
          and Marshall Plan (September 18, 1947)

Predictably, the Soviet Union was not pleased with Truman's speech of March 12. American aid to Greece was distasteful to Moscow, but sending help to Turkey was worse, since that country bordered the Soviet Union and historically had been a problem for Russian foreign policies. The reaction to Secretary Marshall's speech, however, differed. When the European powers responded by calling a meeting at the end of June in Paris to discuss Marshall's offer, Foreign Minister V. M. Molotov appeared with a large entourage of Soviet economic and political experts. He attended the sessions for three days, then angrily left Paris largely because the Western European powers were prepared to offer a package proposal to the United States that would cut across national lines, while the Russians would accept only a program in which national sovereignty was inviolate. Participating in the Marshall Plan would require the Soviets to open much of their economic planning to Western eyes. When Poland and Czechoslovakia indicated interest in the Marshall Plan, Russian pressure forced those two nations to retreat from the Paris talks. At the United Nations in September, the Russian position on the Doctrine and the Marshall Plan was outlined by Andrei Vyshinsky, the Soviet Deputy Minister for Foreign Affairs and Russian spokesman in the U.N. Is it true, as Vyshinsky claims, that the Marshall Plan split Europe into two camps?

The so-called Truman Doctrine and the Marshall Plan are particularly glaring examples of the manner in which the principles of the United Nations are violated, of the way in which the Organization is ignored.

As the experience of the past few months has shown, the proclamation of this doctrine meant that the United States Government has moved toward a direct renunciation of the principles of international collaboration and concerted action by the great Powers and toward attempts to impose its will on other independent states, while at the same time obviously using the economic resources distributed as relief to individual needy nations as an instrument of political pressure. This is clearly proved by the measures taken by the United States Government with regard to Greece and Turkey which ignore and by-pass the United Nations as well as by the measures proposed under

SOURCE. United Nations, General Assembly, *Official Records*, Plenary Meetings, September 18, 1947, pp. 86–88.

the so-called Marshall Plan in Europe. This policy conflicts sharply with the principle expressed by the General Assembly in its resolution of 11 December 1946, which declares that relief supplies to other countries "should . . . at no time be used as a political weapon."

As is now clear, the Marshall Plan constitutes in essence merely a variant of the Truman Doctrine adapted to the conditions of postwar Europe. In bringing forward this plan, the United States Government apparently counted on the cooperation of the Governments of the United Kingdom and France to confront the European countries in need of relief with the necessity of renouncing their inalienable right to dispose of their economic resources and to plan their national economy in their own way. The United States also counted on making all these countries directly dependent on the interests of American monopolies, which are striving to avert the approaching depression by an accelerated export of commodities and capital to Europe. . . .

It is becoming more and more evident to everyone that the implementation of the Marshall Plan will mean placing European countries under the economic and political control of the United States and direct interference by the latter in the internal affairs of those countries.

Moreover, this Plan is an attempt to split Europe into two camps and, with the help of the United Kingdom and France, to complete the formation of a *bloc* of several European countries hostile to the interests of the democratic countries of Eastern Europe and most particularly to the interests of the Soviet Union.

An important feature of this Plan is the attempt to confront the countries of Eastern Europe with a *bloc* of Western European States including Western Germany. The intention is to make use of Western Germany and German heavy industry (the Ruhr) as one of the most important economic bases for American expansion in Europe, in disregard of the national interests of the countries which suffered from German aggression. . . .

43 FROM *J. Edgar Hoover, Harry S. Truman,*
and Henry Steele Commager
The Search for Communists at Home (1947)

The sixth year of the American Century ended not only with the challenge of the Truman Doctrine and the generosity of a Marshall Plan, but with the beginnings of a witch-hunt. That hunt was perhaps inevitable once Americans realized that the planned American Century was becoming a pipe dream. Hopes had been so high, sacrifices had been made, American power in 1945 was indisputably paramount in the military, economic, and ideological realms, yet the results were the communization of Eastern Europe, threatening left-wing movements in Western Europe, uncontrollable civil war in China, and the promise of a protracted cold war. Clearly the fault was neither in our stars nor our system. The fault would therefore have to be found in the way the immense American power had been used. Moving from that premise, an American penchant for personalization and paranoia appeared: a relatively few men must have conspired to restrain United States power and misdirect American diplomacy. That conclusion was false, but it was a mighty tribute to the inability of nearly every American to understand and appreciate that he, no less than a German or Russian, was not immune to tragedy.

Americans know about both tragedy and history (which are not dissimilar), but many believe that neither is relevant to themselves. An example is the tendency to link anti-Communist crusades with only the McCarthyism of the 1950s. That is a historical inaccuracy. The first "Red Scare" occurred in 1919–1920, two years after the Russian Revolution and just as Americans were confronting the frustrations of not having made the "world safe for democracy" in World War I. The second major scare began more than three years before Joseph McCarthy became a household word. The 1945 State Department warning about American Communists (given in Chapter II) formed part of the background. During late 1946 and early 1947, President Truman set in motion preparations for a loyalty investigation of government employees. His decision was motivated in part by a landslide Republican victory in the congressional elections of 1946, and by rousing anti-Communist pronouncements from such noted Americans as J. Edgar Hoover, Director of the Federal Bureau of Investigation. Hoover would play a key role in carrying out Truman's directive of 1947. The President somewhat reluctantly began the program in late 1947, emphasizing, as one of the following selections indicates, that he did not want Federal employees who were "loyal citizens" to feel that they were "the objects of any 'witch hunt.'" The program, however, was loosely drawn and susceptible to the demagogy of headline-seeking politicians. The investigation soon got out of hand. The President never really understood why this occurred. A close reading of the Truman Doctrine suggests one answer: by defining America's Cold War objectives in such terms, Truman had formulated the assumptions that would be used by the witch-hunters of the later McCarthy era. Particularly worthy of thought in this context is the President's claim in volume two of his Memoirs that his foreign policy was not based on mere "containment," but

*aimed at uniting and freeing the entire world. The loyalty program came under im-
mediate attack. Henry Steele Commager, a liberal historian, attacked the loose
wording of the directive and doubted whether Thomas Jefferson could have passed such
a test. The Truman Loyalty Program was a notable result of the search for the American
Century.*

43A   FROM   *J. Edgar Hoover*
Loyal Americans Must Stand Up and Be Counted
(September 30, 1946)

. . . We of the F.B.I. need your help now even more than during the
war years if the battle for a safe and secure America is to be won. Our
enemies are massing their forces on two main fronts. One is the
criminal front. Crime is increasing daily; juvenile delinquency is
shocking; lawlessness is rampant. We are nearer to the days of gang
control than we were a year after World War I. Add to the forces that
account for a serious crime every twenty seconds, day and night, the
other encroaching enemy of America and we have a formidable foe. I
refer to the growing menace of Communism in the United States.

During the past five years, American Communists have made their
deepest inroads upon our national life. In our vaunted tolerance for
all peoples the Communists has found our "Achilles' heel." . . .

The fact that the Communist Party in the United States claims some
100,000 members has lulled many Americans into feeling a false
complacency. I would not be concerned if we were dealing with only
100,000 Communists. The Communists themselves boast that for
every Party member there are ten others ready to do the Party's
work. These include their satellites, their fellow-travelers and their
so-called progressive and phony liberal allies. They have maneuvered
themselves into positions where a few Communists control the
destinies of hundreds who are either willing to be led or have been
duped into obeying the dictates of others.

The average American working man is loyal, patriotic and law-
abiding. He wants security for his family and himself. But in some

SOURCE. J. Edgar Hoover, "Loyal Americans Must Stand Up and Be Counted," *Vital
Speeches of the Day,* **XIII** (October 15, 1946), pp. 10–11. Reprinted by permission of the
publisher.

unions the rank and file find themselves between a Communist pincers, manipulated by a few leaders who have hoodwinked and browbeaten them into a state of submission. Communist labor leaders have sparred for time in their labor deliberations to refer matters of policy to Communist Party headquarters for clearance. . . .

The Communist influence has projected itself into some newspapers, magazines, books, radio and the screen. Some churches, schools, colleges and even fraternal orders have been penetrated, not with the approval of the rank and file but in spite of them. I have been pleased to observe that the Communist attempts to penetrate the American Legion have met with failure. Eternal vigilance will continue to keep your ranks free of shifty, double-crossing Communist destructionists.

We are rapidly reaching the time when loyal Americans must be willing to stand up and be counted. The American Communist Party, despite its claims, is not truly a political party. The Communist Party in this country is not working for the general welfare of all our people—it is working against our people. It is not interested in providing for the common defense. It has for its purpose the shackling of America and its conversion to the Godless, Communist way of life. If it were a political party its adherents could be appealed to by reason. Instead, it is a system of intrigue, actuated by fanaticism. It knows no rules of decency. . . . Let us no longer be misled by their sly propaganda and false preachments on civil liberty. They want civil license to do as they please and, if they get control, liberty for Americans will be but a haunted memory. . . .

We, of this generation, have faced two great menaces in America—Fascism and Communism. Both are materialistic; both are totalitarian; both are anti-religious; both are degrading and inhuman. In fact, they differ little except in name. Communism has bred Fascism and Fascism spawns Communism. Both are the antithesis of American belief in liberty and freedom. If the peoples of other countries want Communism, let them have it, but it has no place in America.

43 B   FROM   *Harry S. Truman*

Disloyal and Subversive Elements Must Be Removed from the
Employ of the Government (November 14, 1947)

I deeply appreciate the willingness of the members of the Loyalty Review Board, established within the Civil Service Commission, to give of their service to that Board. Their acceptance involves real personal sacrifice. At the same time, they will have the satisfaction of knowing that they are contributing to the solution of one of the most difficult problems confronting our Government today.

I believe I speak for all the people of the United States when I say that disloyal and subversive elements must be removed from the employ of the Government. We must not, however, permit employees of the Federal Government to be labeled as disloyal or potentially disloyal to their Government when no valid basis exists for arriving at such a conclusion. The overwhelming majority of Federal employees are loyal citizens who are giving conscientiously of their energy and skills to the United States. I do not want them to fear they are the objects of any "witch hunt." They are not being spied upon; they are not being restricted in their activities. They have nothing to fear from the loyalty program, since every effort has been made to guarantee full protection to those who are suspected of disloyalty. Rumor, gossip, or suspicion will not be sufficient to lead to the dismissal of an employee for disloyalty.

Any person suspected of disloyalty must be served with a written notice of the charges against him in sufficient detail to enable him to prepare his defense. In some unusual situations security considerations may not allow full disclosure.

It would have been possible for the Government to remove disloyal persons merely by serving them with the charges against them and giving them an opportunity to answer those charges. I realize fully, however, the stigma attached to a removal for disloyalty. Accordingly, I have ordered the agencies of the Government, except where a few agencies find it necessary to exercise extraordinary powers granted to them by the Congress, to give hearings to persons who are charged with disloyalty.

Loyalty boards are being set up in each agency for this purpose.

SOURCE. *Public Papers of the Presidents . . . Harry S. Truman . . . 1947* (Washington, D.C.: Government Printing Office, 1963), pp. 489–491.

They are definitely not "kangaroo" courts. The personnel of these boards is being carefully selected by the head of each agency to make sure that they are judicious in temperament and fair-minded. Hearings before the boards will be conducted so as to establish all pertinent facts and to accord the suspected employee every possible opportunity to present his defense. The employee is to be given the right to be accompanied by counsel or a representative of his own choosing.

After the hearing has been completed the loyalty board in each department can recommend the retention or the dismissal of an employee. But the matter does not rest there. The employee may appeal the findings of the loyalty board to the head of the department, who can either approve or disapprove the board's recommendations.

If the head of the department orders the dismissal of the employee, he has still another avenue of appeal: namely, to the Loyalty Review Board within the Civil Service Commission. This Board is composed of outstanding citizens of the United States. These citizens have no ax to grind. They will not be concerned with personalities. Their judgment will be as detached as is humanly possible. . . .

I am looking to the Federal Bureau of Investigation for the conduct of all loyalty investigations which may be necessary in connection with the operation of the program.

I am looking to the Loyalty Review Board to develop standards for the conduct of hearings and the consideration of cases within the various departments and agencies. With the cooperation of the staff of the Civil Service Commission, the Board should make sure that there is complete understanding of and adherence to these standards in all the departments and agencies.

The question of standards is of deep concern to me. Under the Executive order inaugurating this program, provision has been made, for example, for furnishing to the Loyalty Review Board by the Attorney General the name of each foreign or domestic organization, association, movement, group, or combination of persons which he, after appropriate investigation and determination, has designated as totalitarian, fascist, communist, or subversive. The Executive order in turn provides that the Loyalty Review Board shall disseminate such information to all departments and agencies.

This provision of the order has been interpreted by some to mean that any person who at any time happened to belong to one of these organizations would automatically be dismissed from the employ of the Federal Government.

This interpretation completely overlooks the fact that, under the provisions of the Executive order, "the standard for the refusal of employment or the removal from employment in an executive department or agency on grounds relating to loyalty shall be that, on all the evidence, reasonable grounds exist for belief that the person involved is disloyal to the government of the United States."

Membership in an organization is simply one piece of evidence which may or may not be helpful in arriving at a conclusion as to the action which is to be taken in a particular case.

The Government has a great stake in these loyalty proceedings. The Government, as the largest employer in the United States, must be the model of a fair employer. It must guarantee that the civil rights of all employees of the Government shall be protected properly and adequately. It is in this spirit that the loyalty program will be enforced.

43 C FROM *Henry Steele Commager*
Washington Witch-Hunt (April 5, 1947)

It is not improbable that President Truman's executive order on disloyalty in the executive branch was designed to steal the thunder of the Thomas committee or head off such extreme bills as that proposed by Representative Rankin—that it was intended, in short, to furnish some protection to persons in government employment wrongfully accused of disloyalty. If so, it is a pity that it was not more carefully drawn, that it does not more scrupulously observe legal and constitutional proprieties. For as it stands it is an invitation to precisely that kind of witch-hunting which is repugnant to our constitutional system. And as it stands, it should be added, it is liable to instigate persecution not only of radicals by red-baiters but of reactionaries by radicals.

The crucial clauses are in Part V: Standards, and these merit close attention. Most striking is the looseness, the almost unbelievable looseness, with which standards are fixed. Here are the "activities and associations" of an employee which are to be considered as a test of loyalty:

SOURCE. Henry Steele Commager, "Washington Witch-Hunt," *The Nation*, **CLXIV** (April 5, 1947), pp. 385–388. Reprinted by permission of the publisher.

"Membership in, affiliation with, or sympathetic association with any foreign or domestic organization, association, movement, group or combination of persons, designated by the Attorney General as totalitarian, fascist, Communist, or subversive, or as having adopted a policy of advocating or approving the commission of acts of force or violence to deny other persons their rights under the Constitution of the United States, or as seeking to alter the form of government of the United States by unconstitutional means."

Note first how all-embracing these terms are. It is not only membership in or affiliation with subversive organizations that is proscribed, but "sympathetic association" with them. What is sympathetic association, and how it is to de distinguished from unsympathetic association? Is a member of the Democratic Party in New York sympathetically or unsympathetically associated with the Democratic Party of Mississippi, which denies Negroes their rights under the Constitution of the United States? Note, too, the connection—it is difficult to use more precise word—that is made suspect. It is not only membership and so forth in actual organizations but membership in and sympathetic association with a "movement" or a "group or combination of persons." What is a movement? Is the Wave of the Future a movement? Is anti-Semitism a movement? Is hostility to organized labour a movement?

Here is the doctrine of guilt by association with a vengeance. For almost a hundred and fifty years American law labored under the handicap of being unable to prove guilt by association. The Alien Registration Act of 1940, directed against aliens and enacted under pressure of war, for the first time wrote that odious doctrine into American law. Now, apparently, it is here to stay. Guilt is no longer to be personal, no longer to depend upon overt acts. It is an infectious thing, to be achieved by mere "sympathetic association" with others presumed to be guilty, or even with "movements" presumed to be subversive.

Nor is consolation to be found in the designation of the Attorney General as the person to classify organizations and movements as subversive. An intelligent Attorney General, an open-minded and tolerant one, would doubtless use this broad power with discretion. But how would it be used by a Stanton, who double-crossed his President; how would it be used by a Richard Olney, who smashed the Pullman strike; how would it be used by an A. Mitchell Palmer, who rounded up the "reds" ...? What guaranty is there that J. Edgar

Hoover may not some day be Attorney General, Hoover who recently asserted that "so-called progressives and phony liberals" are little better than Communists? The same pervasive and pernicious looseness of phrasing characterizes another of the standards set up in this section. For one of the tests of loyalty is "performing or attempting to perform his duties, or otherwise acting, so as to serve the interests of another government in preference to the interests of the United States." What is "otherwise acting" so as to serve the interests of some government other than the United States—and who is to decide? It is worth noting, in passing, that much this same test was enacted before, in the Logan act of 1798—and failed. . . .

But let us turn to some of the possible applications of this extraordinary order. What organizations, associations, movements, or groups, after all, may be said to be embraced in the esoteric phrases of Part V? Communist and fascist are, perhaps, obvious enough, though "totalitarian" takes a bit of defining. But what of others that "advocate or approve" the commission of acts of force to deny persons their rights under the Constitution or to alter the form of government? The Ku Klux Klan is obviously one of these, and we may confidently expect that it will be so designated by the Attorney General and that all its members in government service will be promptly charged with disloyalty.

What shall we say, what may we expect, for other organizations? Is membership in the Democratic Party, or "sympathetic association" with it, an indication of disloyalty? Assuredly, that party countenances the use of force to deprive Southern Negroes of their rights under the Constitution. What of membership in labor unions? Several of them have, notoriously, denied to non-members or to the public their constitutional rights. . . . Nor should we forget that numerous Congressmen have again and again asserted that various unions were Communist-dominated. Clearly they must know what they are talking about, and clearly all who associate with or sympathize with these unions are guilty through association. . . . Or, to turn to government employees, is service with the F.B.I. to be an indication of disloyalty if that agency attempts, as it clearly wishes, to deny Communists their constitutional right of freedom of speech and of assembly?

Fortunately for those who tremble for the safety of the Republic, the dragnet is to be spread widely enough to catch even those whose sympathetic association with subversive groups or movements is not clear. For all those who seek "to alter the form of government of the

United States by unconstitutional means" are equally subject to the Attorney General's disapproval. What are "unconstitutional means"? It is a bit difficult to know what may be considered unconstitutional in the future, but perhaps recourse to the past will clarify the issue. Clearly, all those who carried out the Congressional mandate, in 1862, to abolish slavery in the territories were guilty of this crime, for under the Dred Scott decision the act of 1862 was unconstitutional. Even more clearly, all officers who executed the First Reconstruction Act, and its amendments, were equally guilty, for these acts were palpably unconstitutional, and, no less palpably, they altered the American form of government.

An application of Mr. Truman's executive order to the past would, indeed, greatly have simplified our history. An order of this kind would have disposed of that dangerous radical Andrew Jackson, who not once but twice flouted the Supreme Court, and of Jackson's Attorney General, Taney, later Chief Justice, who aided and abetted him. . . . It would have embarrassed that subversive executive Abraham Lincoln, who illegally, according to Chief Justice Taney, suspended the writ of habeas corpus, thus denying to John Merryman rights guaranteed to him by the Constitution. It might have put that dangerous agitator Theodore Roosevelt in his place—Roosevelt who, according to President Taft, illegally withdrew public lands from entry, thus denying persons their constitutional rights to homesteads. And whatever we may think of more recent situations, such an order— had it but been effective in time—would inevitably have disposed of Mr. Truman's trouble-making predecessor, Thomas Jefferson. For Jefferson "sympathetically associated" with Jacobin clubs, Jefferson "sympathetically" joined combinations to nullify Congressional acts, Jefferson affiliated with a party which worked a "revolution" in 1800, and—worst of all—Jefferson openly announced that "the tree of liberty must be refreshed from time to time with the blood of patriots and martyrs."

BIBLIOGRAPHY

There are a number of excellent general works that cover all or most of the 1939–1947 era: Gaddis Smith, *American Diplomacy During the Second World War, 1941–1945* (New York, 1965) is a superb short account; the best detailed treatment is William H. McNeill, *America, Britain, and Russia* (London, 1953) which takes the story down through 1946; Herbert Feis' three works, *Churchill, Roosevelt, Stalin* (Princeton, 1957), *Between War and Peace: The Potsdam Conference*, and *The Atomic Bomb and the End of World War II* (Princeton, 1966); Winston Churchill's history of the Second World War, especially *The Grand Alliance* (Boston, 1950) and *Triumph and Tragedy* (Boston, 1953); Desmond Donnelly, *Struggle for the World* (New York, 1965); and Norman Graebner (ed.), *An Uncertain Tradition, American Secretaries of State in the Twentieth Century* (New York, 1961). William Appleman Williams, *The Tragedy of American Diplomacy* (New York, 1962) opened many new insights into twentieth-century American diplomacy; Lloyd Gardner, *Economic Aspects of New Deal Diplomacy* (Madison, Wisc., 1964) is the best synthesis of the entire 1933–1945 period, and Gardner's *Architects of Illusion* (Chicago, 1970) is the best work covering the entire 1940s; Denna Frank Fleming, *The Cold War and Its Origins, 1917–1960*, 2 vols. (Garden City, N.Y., 1961) provides the details for the so-called "revisionist" view of American and Russian war-time diplomacy. The best, most detailed, and most provocative account on the three pivotal years is Gabriel Kolko, *The Politics of War. The World and United States Foreign Policy, 1943–1945* (New York, 1968).

Many of the studies of war-time diplomacy climax with the 1945 events, although providing good background on American-Russian-British relations during the conflict: John L. Snell, *Wartime Origins of the East-West Dilemma over Germany* (New Orleans, 1959); Robert E. Sherwood, *Roosevelt and Hopkins* (New York, 1948), particularly helpful on the 1943–1945 conferences; E. P. Penrose, *Economic Planning for the Peace* (Princeton, 1953); Robert Divine, *Second Chance: The Triumph of Internationalism in America During World War II* (New York, 1967), a fine account of political maneuvering within the United States in regards to the United Nations and collective security issues; Allen Dulles, *The Secret Surrender* (New York, 1966) on the effects of the Italian surrender negotiations upon Soviet-American relations; Gar Alperovitz, *Atomic Diplomacy* (New York, 1965), a detailed study of 1945; the first volume of Harry S. Truman's *Memoirs* (Garden City, N.Y., 1955), to be supplemented by Barton J. Bernstein and Allen J. Matusow, *The Truman Administration: A Documentary History* (New York, 1966); and Richard N. Gardner, *Sterling-Dollar Diplomacy* (Oxford, 1956), a superb account of Anglo-American relations with particular emphasis on the British loan negotiations. Absolutely essential in understanding the diplomacy of these years are two series published by the U.S. Department of State: *U.S. Department of State Bulletin*, and the volumes in *Foreign Relations of the United States*, which in their coverage of the diplomatic correspondence are now down through 1946 and are supplemented by special volumes on the Yalta and Potsdam Conferences.

Besides Truman's *Memoirs* mentioned above, there is a wealth of auto-biographical material available for these years: Robert Murphy, *Diplomat Among Warriors* (New York, 1964); Arthur H. Vandenberg, *Private Papers* (Boston, 1952), especially good on the United Nations and the Soviets; James F. Forrestal, *The Forrestal Diaries*, edited by Walter Millis (New York, 1951), a key primary source which may be supplemented with Arnold A. Rogow's controversial biography, *James Forrestal* (New York, 1963); James F. Byrnes, *Speaking Frankly* (New York, 1947); and George F. Kennan, *Memoirs, 1925–1950* (Boston, 1967); Dean Acheson, *Present At The Creation* (New York, 1969).

Besides the Divine volume, *Second Chance*, noted above, the following are helpful in understanding the internal American debate and the domestic repurcussions of the Cold War: two essays by Barton Bernstein, who also edited *Towards a New Past*; *Dissenting Essays in American History* (New York, 1968); essays by Bernstein and Athan Theoharis in *The Truman Years* (Chicago, 1970), edited by Bernstein; Clifton Brock, *Americans for Democratic Action*; Cabell Phillips, *The Truman Presidency* (New York, 1966), the most helpful biography; David A. Shannon, *The Decline of American Communism* (New York, 1959).

On Soviet foreign policy, besides the Djilas and Molotov volumes noted in the text, the following provide good surveys: Isaac Deutscher, *Stalin*, revised edition (New York, 1967); George Frost Kennan, *Russia and the West Under Lenin and Stalin*; Philip E. Moseley, *The Kremlin and World Politics* (New York, 1960), helpful although most of the essays are on the post-1947 period; Raymond L. Garthoff, *Soviet Military Policy* (New York, 1966); Alexander Dallin, *The Soviet Union at the United Nations* (New York, 1962); Walter Z. Laqueur, *Russia and Germany* (London, 1965); Margaret Dewar, *Soviet Trade with Eastern Europe, 1945–1949* (London, 1953). Adam B. Ulam, *Expansion and Coexistence, The History of Soviet Foreign Policy, 1917–1967* (New York, 1968) is the best account of the subject.